Religion 2
for Young Catholics

Nihil Obstat given at Scranton, Pennsylvania on the 25th day of October, 2000, by Monsignor David Bohr, the Censor Librorum.

Imprimatur given at Scranton, Pennsylvania, on the 3rd day of November, 2000, by the Most Reverend James C. Timlin, D.D., Bishop of Scranton.

The *nihil obstat* and *imprimatur* are official declarations that a book or pamphlet is free of doctrinal or moral error. No implication is contained therein that those who granted the *nihil obstat* or *imprimatur* agree with the contents, opinions, or statements expressed.

The Seton Catholic Family Catechism Series
A Religion Series for Children Educated at Home by Their Parents

Written by the Seton Home Study School Staff
Executive Editor: Dr. Mary Kay Clark
Editors: Seton Staff

Seton Home Study School
1350 Progress Drive
Front Royal, VA 22630
540-636-9990
540-636-1602 fax

For more information, visit us on the Web at http://www.setonhome.org.
Contact us by e-mail at info@setonhome.org.

ISBN: 978-1-60704-015-6

Cover: St. Ann showing the Sacred Scriptures to Mary

Dedicated to the
Sacred Heart of Jesus

Acknowledgements:

Thank you to all the Seton staff who have worked to make this book suitable for children being taught at home by their parents.

We especially thank Jesus in His Most Sacred Heart for directing our writing, editing, illustrating, and desktop publishing.

We thank His Most Blessed Mother Mary, and His foster-father on earth, St. Joseph, both of whom were perfect parents who taught their perfect Son, Jesus, at home.

Foreword to Parents

This text is intended to help children at about the second grade level to learn their Catholic Faith from their parents at home.

The text consists of thirty-six units or weeks, to be about equivalent to a typical "school" year. Four review units are included: units nine, eighteen, twenty-seven, and thirty-six.

Some of the review questions found on Day 4 of each week may be preceded by an asterisk. This indicates that the question and answer are taken directly from the Baltimore Catechism.

It might surprise parents to see how much we have included in a catechism for a young child. We are following the directives of the General Catechetical Directory from the Vatican, as well as following the new Catechism of the Catholic Church.

Both the Directory and the new Catechism emphasize the importance of teaching all of the basic truths of the Faith each year: the Creed, the Commandments, the Sacraments, and Prayers. At the same time, the Directory states that the lessons are to be presented at a level appropriate to the age of the child.

Some lessons will be more detailed than others, but all the Sacraments and all the Commandments will be taught.

A Note on the Stained Glass Illustrations in This Book

The stained glass windows depicted in this book are found in churches all over the world. There are windows from churches in Chicago and New York and even Australia. France, of course, is famous for the stained glass in its Gothic cathedrals.

Stained glass has a long history in Catholic art. Although it existed in early Christian times, stained glass reached the pinnacle of fine art during the Medieval period of the twelfth and thirteenth centuries, when the Cathedral of Chartres was built. The Chartres Cathedral, perhaps the most renowned of all churches for its extraordinary stained glass windows, has a massive window depicting the life of Our Lord. The size of this stained-glass window is over 250 square feet!

Stained glass was styled to allow beams of light to pass through, giving the effect of brilliant jewels surrounding the high walls of the enormous cathedrals of long ago. Because of the constant change of light throughout the day and the seasons of the year, the stained glass depictions were ever changing, even from one minute to the next.

The aesthetical quality of stained glass served the very practical purpose of teaching catechism in pictures. Scenes from the Bible and the lives of the saints were the predominant themes in colored glass.

The oldest stained glass depicted in this book is from the end of the fifteenth century. The newest glass is from the 1930s, which was strongly influenced by the "Art Deco" style of that era. Examples of stained glass have been chosen from those times because they have a more realistic interpretation of events than glass made in other periods. Glass before the end of the 1400s was more two-dimensional and lacked much of the color that future generations of this artwork would have. The glass of those times was predominantly blue, with the Cathedral of Chartres having some of the finest examples of stained glass of that time.

The stained glass created after 1940 is more "modern" in its style, and people are portrayed in unrealistic ways that would be difficult for second grade children to understand.

Most of the Catholic churches built in the United States at the end of the nineteenth century have extraordinary examples of priceless stained glass. Stained glass almost became a dying art because of the church renovations of the last forty years. Fortunately, however, highly-skilled artisans are now resurrecting the art form. Consider visiting some of the 100–150-year-old churches in your area for a special field trip. See *The Official Catholic Directory* to learn when a church was built.

We hope that through the introduction of the examples in this book, your child will develop an appreciation for the beauty of stained glass.

Contents

PRAYERS

The Sign of the Cross

In the Name of the Father,
and of the Son,
and of the Holy Spirit.
Amen.

The Lord's Prayer

Our Father, Who art in Heaven,
hallowed be Thy name.
Thy Kingdom come,
Thy Will be done on earth
as it is in Heaven.

Give us this day our daily bread.
And forgive us our trespasses
as we forgive those
who trespass against us.
And lead us not into temptation,
but deliver us from evil.
Amen.

The Hail Mary

Hail Mary, full of grace,
the Lord is with thee,
Blessed art thou among women,
and blessed is the Fruit of thy womb, Jesus.

Holy Mary, Mother of God,
pray for us sinners,
now and at the hour of our death.
Amen.

Glory Be

Glory be to the Father,
and to the Son,
and to the Holy Spirit,

as it was in the beginning,
is now,
and ever shall be,
world without end.
Amen.

The Apostles' Creed

I believe in God
the Father Almighty,
Creator of Heaven and earth.
And in Jesus Christ,
His only Son, Our Lord,
Who was conceived by the Holy Spirit,
born of the Virgin Mary,
suffered under Pontius Pilate,
was crucified, died, and was buried.
He descended into Hell.
The third day He arose again from the dead.
He ascended into Heaven,
sits at the right hand of God,
the Father Almighty.
From thence He shall come
to judge the living and the dead.

I believe in the Holy Spirit,
the Holy Catholic Church,
the Communion of Saints,
the forgiveness of sins,
the resurrection of the body,
and life everlasting.
Amen.

Prayer to My Guardian Angel

Angel of God
My guardian dear,
To whom God's love
Entrusts me here.

Ever this day,

Be at my side,
To light and guard,
To rule and guide.
Amen.

Act of Contrition

O my God, I am heartily sorry
for having offended Thee.
And I detest all my sins,
because of Thy just punishments,
but most of all
because they offend Thee, my God,
Who art all good
and deserving of all my love.

I firmly resolve
with the help of Thy grace,
To sin no more,
and to avoid the near occasions of sin.
Amen.

Blessing before Meals

Bless us, O Lord,
and these Thy gifts,
which we are about to receive,
from Thy bounty
through Christ our Lord.
Amen.

Blessing after Meals

We give Thee thanks
for all Thy benefits,
Almighty God,
Who lives and reigns forever.
Amen.

May the souls of the faithful departed,
through the mercy of God,
rest in peace.
Amen.

Dedicated to St. Thérèse, the Little Flower

The Making of a Saint

In chapter two of her autobiography, *The Story of a Soul*, St. Thérèse tells the story of events that happened when she was six and seven years old. Those events give us a clear picture of how a family of today can raise a saint. Like all of us home-schooling families, the Martin family made conscious efforts at developing the spiritual life through specific devotions and activities for the children. The following are some excerpts from chapter two.

"Every morning ... I said my prayers kneeling at your side. Afterwards I had a reading lesson. 'Heaven' [in French] was the first word I read ... Every afternoon I went for a walk with Daddy and paid a visit to the Blessed Sacrament, going to a different church every day. It was during one of these walks that I entered the Carmel chapel for the first time. Daddy showed me the choir grille and said that nuns lived behind it ... I loved growing flowers in the bit of garden given me by Daddy, and I enjoyed decorating little altars I made in a niche in the wall ...

"Sometimes I tried to fish with my little line, but I preferred to sit alone on the grass amid the flowers. Then I used to think very deeply, and though I knew nothing of meditation, my soul entered into a true state of prayer ... The faint music filled me with a gentle melancholy. Earth seemed a place of exile and I dreamt of Heaven ... we heard the rumbling of a storm. Lightning shot through the lowering clouds, and I saw a thunderbolt strike nearby. I wasn't a bit frightened. Indeed, I was full of delight, for it seemed that God was very near to me.

"During my walks with Daddy, he loved to let me give alms to the poor people we met. Once we met a poor old man. Although I was then only six, I said to myself: 'I will pray for my poor old man at my First Communion.' I kept my promise five years later, and I hope that God has answered the prayer He inspired me to offer Him for one of the Church's suffering members.

"Marie said I was too young to go to the May devotions. I stayed at home and made my devotions with her, in front of my little altar which I had decorated myself. Everything on it was so small—candlesticks and flower vases and such—that a couple of wax matches lit it perfectly. One evening, as we were going to begin our prayers, I said to her: Will you begin the Memorare? I am going to light the matches ...

"I made my first confession soon afterwards. What a wonderful memory I have of it! How carefully you prepared me! You told me I was going to confess my sins not to a man but to God Himself. I was so absolutely convinced of this that I made my confession full of great faith and I even asked you if I should tell Father that I loved him with all my heart since it was God I was going to speak to in his person ... After that I went to confession on every big feast day, and every time I went it was a real feast for me.

"Feast days!...I loved feast days so much ... they seemed like days spent in Heaven. Best of all, I loved when the Blessed Sacrament was carried in procession, for it gave me such joy to scatter flowers beneath the feet of God. But before letting them fall there, I used to throw them as high as I could and nothing delighted me more than to see my rose petals touch the Monstrance.

"Whenever the preacher mentioned St. Teresa, Daddy would lean over and whisper: 'Listen carefully, my little queen. He is speaking of your holy patron.'...I used to look more at Daddy than at the preacher because I could read so much in his noble face ... As he heard the eternal truths, he seemed as if he had already left the earth ... As we walked home, I gazed with delight at the stars shining above. There was one group in particular which filled me with joy, for I noticed that it was in the shape of the letter T. I pointed it out to Daddy and told him that my name was written in Heaven. I didn't want to see any more of this dreary world and asked him to guide me. Then, without looking where I was going, I kept my face turned up to the starry sky.

"I loved sitting on Daddy's knee ... as he recited religious poems. Then we all said our evening prayers together ...You carried me up to bed and I used to say: 'Have I been good today? Are the little angels going to watch over me?' You always said yes or I should have spent the whole night in tears.

"I've often wondered how you were able to bring me up with so much love and yet not spoil me. You never passed over a single fault, but you never reproached me without good cause.

"I was six or seven when Daddy took us to Trouville. I shall never forget the impression the sea made on me. I could not take my eyes from it. The majestic roaring of its waves filled me with a sense of the power and majesty of God ... I sat with you on a rock one evening at the time when the sun seems to sink into the vastness of the ocean at the end of a path of light. I gazed at this path of light and saw it as a symbol of the grace which lit the way along which the little white-sailed skiff would journey. Sitting by your side, I resolved never to let my soul wander from the gaze of Jesus, so that it could sail peacefully towards the shores of Heaven." (From *The Autobiography of St. Thérèse of Lisieux: The Story of a Soul,* New York: Doubleday & Company, 1957: pp. 30-38.)

First Quarter

The Blessed Trinity and Creation

In this book, called a catechism, we are going to learn about God. You already have learned about God from your mother and father. We can learn about God from the Catholic Church and the Bible, God's holy book.

We know that there is only one God. From the Church and the Bible, we know there are three Persons in one God.

The three Persons in one God are God the Father, God the Son, and God the Holy Spirit (sometimes called the Holy Ghost). We call the three Persons in one God the Blessed Trinity.

There is only one God, but there are three Persons in one God. We cannot understand this. It is a big mystery.

Jesus, the Son of God, told us about the Blessed Trinity. When we go to Heaven, we will more fully understand the Blessed Trinity.

St. Patrick explained the Blessed Trinity to the Irish people. He said the Blessed Trinity is like a three-leaf clover. There is one clover but it has three leaves in one clover.

God is three Persons. But He is still only One God.

1. There are _____ Persons in one God.

2. We call this mystery the _____ _____.

3. St. Patrick explained the Blessed Trinity with a three-leaf

   _____.

4. There is only _____ God.

1

Long ago, before Jesus was born, God appeared many times to the holy prophets and leaders. We read about this in the first part of the Bible.

God appeared in a burning bush to Moses. Later, God appeared to Moses on a mountain and gave him the Ten Commandments. God appeared to Abraham and his wife Sarah.

In the second part of the Bible, we learn about God the Son. God the Son is Jesus Christ. We learn about the love of Jesus for each one of us. Jesus worked many miracles, helping people, curing them of sickness.

We learn about the Holy Spirit from Jesus. The Holy Spirit appeared above the head of Jesus when He was baptized.

Jesus told His apostles that He would send the Holy Spirit to guide the Church. The Holy Spirit appeared over the heads of the apostles on Pentecost Sunday.

1. God appeared in a burning bush to _____.

2. Jesus worked many _____.

3. We learn about the Holy Spirit from _____.

4. The _____ _____ appeared above the head of Jesus when He was baptized.

We learn about Creation from the Bible. Creation means something made out of nothing. Only God can make something out of nothing.

God is the Creator of man and of all things. This means that He is the One Who made all things out of nothing.

In the beginning, God created the whole world out of nothing. God created the heavens and the earth, the sun and moon and stars.

God created the land and the seas and the oceans. God created the fish and the birds and the animals. God created the world and all the beautiful things in it.

God is good. He is so good that He wanted to share His goodness. He created people so they could go to Heaven and be happy with Him forever.

We should thank God for everything He has given us.

**"For flowers that bloom about our feet
For tender grass so fresh and sweet,
For song of bird and hum of bee,
For all things fair we hear or see,
For blue of stream and blue of sky,
For pleasant shade of branches high,
For fragrant air and cooling breeze,
For beauty of the blooming trees,
God, our Father, we thank Thee."**

1. _____ means something made out of nothing.

2. In the beginning, God _____ the world out of nothing.

3. God is so good, He wanted to share His _____.

3

The Blessed Trinity and Creation: Review Questions

*1. Is there only one God?
Yes, there is only one God.

*2. How many Persons are there in God?
In God, there are three Persons: the Father, the Son, and the Holy Spirit.

*3. What do we call the three Persons in one God?
We call the three Persons in one God the Blessed Trinity.

*4. How do we know that there are three Persons in one God?
We know that there are three Persons in one God because we have God's word for it.

5. Who is God the Son?
God the Son is Jesus Christ, the second Person of the Blessed Trinity.

6. Who is the third Person of the Blessed Trinity?
God the Holy Spirit (or Holy Ghost) is the third Person of the Blessed Trinity.

7. What does "creation" mean?
"Creation" means something made out of nothing.

8. Who is the Creator?
God is the Creator.

The Angels

God is so good, He wanted to share His goodness. So God created angels to share His love and goodness. He created angels to live with Him in Heaven.

God created angels before He created the world on earth. The angels were happy loving God in God's beautiful home in Heaven.

Angels are not like people. Angels are pure spirits. They have a mind and a will, but they do not have bodies as we do. God made the angels with very bright minds and free wills. God gave the angels great knowledge.

Then, a terrible thing happened. One of the angels, Lucifer, decided He did not want to obey God.

Lucifer joined with some other angels who also did not want to obey God. These angels were disobedient to God. They committed the first sin.

Because these angels committed a terrible sin against God, they could not stay in Heaven. So God created a place of fire called Hell. The bad angels were sent to Hell. By the power of God, Michael the Archangel cast Lucifer into Hell. Lucifer's name was changed. He was no longer called the "light bearer." He is now called "Satan," which means "the enemy."

1. God created _____ to share His love and goodness.

2. Angels do not have bodies; they are pure _____.

3. The bad angels committed the first _____.

We read about angels in the Bible. God loved the good angels. God knows the good angels love Him.

Angels in Heaven love and adore God. The angels praise God all the time.

Some angels are messengers for God. God sent the angel Gabriel to Mary to ask her to be the mother of Jesus. God sent the angel Raphael to Tobias to help him find a wife.

Angels were messengers to the shepherds in Bethlehem. An angel led Saint Peter out of prison.

Some angels are guardian angels. God gives every person a guardian angel. There are so many guardian angels that only God knows how many there are!

1. The angels in Heaven _____ God all the time.

2. Some angels are _____ for God.

3. God gives each person a _____ _____.

God gives each of us a guardian angel. Our guardian angels are always with us even though we cannot see them. Our guardian angels help us not to sin. They also protect us.

We have angels always with us to help us choose to be good. We should pray to our guardian angel to help us when we are in danger. We should ask our guardian angel to help us do our work.

Our guardian angel loves us.

Say this prayer every day:

**"Angel of God,
My guardian dear,
To whom God's love
Entrusts me here.
Ever this day
Be at my side,
To light and guard,
To rule and guide.
Amen."**

1. Our guardian angels help us choose to be _____.

2. Our guardian angels also _____ us.

Angels: Review Questions

1. Why did God create the angels?
God created the angels to share His love and goodness with them.

2. What are angels?
Angels are pure spirits; they have no bodies.

3. Who is the leader of the bad angels who were disobedient to God?
Lucifer is the leader of the bad angels who were disobedient to God.

4. Who is the good archangel who cast Lucifer into Hell by the power of God?
By the power of God, Michael the Archangel cast Lucifer into Hell.

5. What do angels do?
Angels praise God, act as messengers for God, and serve as guardian angels.

6. What are some things which your guardian angel does for you?
My guardian angel helps me choose to be good. He helps me when I am in danger. He helps me with my work.

God Made the World and Man

God never had a beginning. He always was, and He always will be. He can never die.

Everything else had a beginning. We had a beginning. But God did not have a beginning.

God is all-good and all-loving.

God is all-powerful. He can do all things.

God can create things out of nothing.

God is everywhere. God's home is Heaven, but He is everywhere.

God knows all things. God knows everything people say and do and think. God knows all our innermost thoughts and secrets.

God is perfectly happy, but God wants to share His happiness and His goodness. He wants to share His heavenly home.

God created angels to share His love and goodness. He also created people to share His love and goodness.

1. God never had a _____.

2. God is perfectly _____, but wants to _____ His happiness.

3. God is all-good and all-_____.

4. God is all-_____. He can do all things.

5. God can _____ things out of nothing.

God is love and goodness! He wants to share Himself all the time. God created angels first to share His love and goodness. Then God made people to share His love and goodness.

When God created angels, He created millions of angels. When God created people, He created one man.

God made Adam, the first man, from the dirt of the earth.

Then God breathed His breath into Adam. This gave Adam life. It gave him a soul. Because of his soul, Adam had a bright mind and free will.

God put Adam in a beautiful garden called Paradise. Adam loved the beautiful world God created.

After some time passed, God made a woman, Eve, from a rib of Adam. Adam and Eve lived happily in Paradise. They were perfectly happy because they were full of love for God.

1. God made people to share His love and _____.

2. God made the first man, who was named _____.

3. God's breath gave Adam life and a _____.

4. God made Eve from a _____ of Adam.

5. Adam and Eve lived in a garden called _____.

Adam and Eve were very happy in Paradise.

They are the parents of the whole human race. They are the first mother and father of all the people in the world.

Adam and Eve loved God.

God filled their souls with divine grace. They had no sin on their souls.

They were holy and happy. They were very intelligent. God gave them all the knowledge they needed. They did not have to study or learn.

Adam and Eve would never die. They could go to Heaven without dying.

1. Adam and Eve are the _____ of the whole human race.

2. God gave them all the _____ they needed. They did not have to study or learn

3. God filled their souls with divine _____.

4. Adam and Eve were _____ and happy.

5. Adam and Eve could go to _____ without dying.

God Made Man: Review Questions

*1. Did God have a beginning?
No, God had no beginning. He always was.

*2. Will God always be?
Yes, God will always be.

*3. Where is God?
God is everywhere.

*4. Why did God make you?
God made me to show His goodness and to make me happy with Him in Heaven.

5. Who were the first man and woman God made?
Adam and Eve were the first man and woman God made.

6. Are Adam and Eve the parents of the human race?
Yes, Adam and Eve are the parents of the human race.

Adam and Eve and Their Fall

Adam and Eve were the first man and woman made by God.

Adam loved Eve very much. Eve loved Adam very much. They both loved God. They were very happy together in Paradise.

They enjoyed Paradise. They ate all kinds of delicious fruit, sweet and juicy, from the trees.

There were four beautiful clear flowing rivers in the Garden. Two were named the Tigris and the Euphrates, which you can find on a map today.

The animals were gentle and friendly. The birds were all different colors, shining brightly.

It was never too hot in the Garden of Paradise, and it was never cold. The weather was always perfect.

All kinds of flowers of every color, shade, and tint surrounded Adam and Eve. The scents from the flowers gave off the most heavenly perfume!

1. Adam and Eve ate _____ in Paradise.

2. Two of the rivers in the Garden of Paradise were the _____ and the Euphrates.

3. The animals were gentle and _____.

4. The birds were all different _____.

5. The weather was always _____.

Adam and Eve lived in the beautiful garden called Paradise.

God gave them one command. God told Adam and Eve: "Of every tree in Paradise you may eat. But of the tree of knowledge of good and evil, you shall not eat. For if in any day you do eat of it, you shall die."

God commanded this so that Adam and Eve could show that they loved Him and would obey Him.

Adam and Eve knew they must not eat of the fruit of the tree of knowledge of good and evil.

God allowed the bad angel, Satan, to appear as a serpent to Eve. Satan told her that if she ate of the forbidden fruit, she would not die.

Satan told Eve that God did not want her to eat of the forbidden fruit because then she would become like God.

Eve looked at the forbidden fruit, and suddenly it seemed

"good to eat, and fair to the eyes, and delightful to behold," says the Bible.

Sin is disobeying God.

Eve disobeyed God. Eve sinned.

1. God gave Adam and Eve one _____.

2. Satan told Eve that she would not _____ if she ate the fruit.

3. Sin is _____ God.

14

Sin is disobeying God. Eve was tempted to sin by the devil. The devil told Eve she would be like God.

Eve took some of the forbidden fruit from the tree and ate it. "She took of the fruit thereof, and did eat," it says in the Bible.

Then Eve went to Adam. She gave him some of the fruit to eat. Adam knew it was wrong. Adam knew he should obey God. It says in the Bible that Eve "gave to her husband, who did eat."

Adam committed the sin of disobedience. We call Adam's sin Original Sin.

Then, God came walking in the Garden of Paradise.

"Adam and his wife hid themselves from the face of the Lord God, amidst the trees of Paradise." Adam and Eve were very ashamed and sorry for disobeying God.

Disobeying God is always evil and never brings happiness.

1. Adam and Eve disobeyed God by eating the _____ of the forbidden tree.

2. Adam and Eve hid themselves from God because they were

_____ of their sin.

Adam and Eve: Review Questions

1. What was the command God gave Adam and Eve?
God commanded Adam and Eve not to eat of the fruit of the tree of knowledge of good and evil.

2. Who appeared to Eve as a serpent?
The devil, Satan, appeared to Eve as a serpent.

3. What did Satan tell Eve?
Satan told Eve that if she ate the forbidden fruit, she would not die, but would be like God.

*4. Who committed the first sin on earth?
Our first parents, Adam and Eve, committed the first sin on earth.

5. What do we call the first sin?
We call the first sin original sin.

6. Were Adam and Eve sorry for their sin?
Adam and Eve were ashamed and sorry for their sin. They tried to hide from God.

Original Sin

Adam and Eve were our first parents. God commanded them to obey Him, but Adam and Eve disobeyed God. Sin appeared on earth for the first time.

As soon as Adam and Eve sinned, grace left their souls. They lost the gift of grace.

They lost their bright minds. They could not think as quickly as before.

They lost their gift of knowledge. They could not remember many things God had told them.

They lost the gift of perfect health. Now they would suffer pain and sickness. Now they would die.

They were driven out of Paradise. God even closed the gates of Heaven! Adam and Eve would not be able to enter Heaven. No one can enter Heaven with sin on his soul.

1. Adam and Eve _____ God.

2. When Adam and Eve sinned, they lost the gift of _____.

3. They were driven out of _____.

4. Adam and Eve lost the gift of perfect _____, and would suffer pain and sickness.

5. No one can enter Heaven with _____ on his soul.

Adam and Eve committed the first sin of the human race. This first sin is called original sin.

Adam and Eve still loved God. They were sorry for their sin. They wept in sorrow. They were sorry they offended God. God is good. He loved Adam and Eve even after they sinned.

Adam was the first parent of the human race. When Adam disobeyed God, he hurt all the people born in all the years to come. All people are born with Adam's original sin on their souls.

We are all born without God's grace. As little babies, we are born with original sin.

All of us sometimes want to sin. All of us suffer sickness, pain, and death of our bodies. All of us must work hard to learn. All of us must work hard for our food and clothing.

We suffer all these things because we are born with original sin on our souls.

QUEEN OF MISSIONS

1. All of us are born with _____ _____ on our souls.

2. This means that we are born without God's _____.

Adam and Eve disobeyed God's command. They ate the forbidden fruit. They committed the first sin of mankind.

Right away, grace left their souls. No longer did they have special intelligence. No longer did they have grace to be good. They became sad and unhappy.

God put them out of Paradise. God put angels with flaming swords in front of the entrance. Worst of all, God shut the gates to Heaven.

Adam and Eve no longer had grace in their souls. Without grace, they could not go to Heaven.

This sin of Adam, the head of the entire human race, is passed down to all of us. This sin we inherit is called original sin. It was the first sin of mankind.

All people are born with original sin. Only one person never had original sin. The Blessed Virgin Mary, the mother of Jesus, never had original sin.

1. When Adam and Eve sinned, _____ left their souls.

2. The Blessed Virgin Mary never had _____ _____.

3. _____ with flaming swords guarded the Garden of Paradise.

Original Sin : Review Questions

1. What happened to Adam and Eve when they disobeyed God?
They lost the gifts of grace and were driven out of Paradise.

2. What did God do when Adam and Eve sinned?
When Adam and Eve sinned, God closed the gates of Heaven to them and to all mankind.

*3. Is this sin passed on to us from Adam?
Yes, this sin is passed on to us from Adam.

*4. What is this sin in us called?
This sin in us is called original sin.

*5. Was anyone ever free from original sin?
The Blessed Virgin Mary, the Mother of Jesus, was free from original sin.

6. What do we now suffer as a result of original sin?
As a result of original sin, we now suffer sickness, pain, and death of our bodies.

God Promises a Savior

God loved Adam and Eve. God loves all of us. God wants all of us to be in Heaven with Him.

God wanted Adam and Eve to be in Heaven with Him. God wants all the people born after Adam and Eve to be in Heaven with Him. But because of their sins, they could not go to Heaven. So God made a wonderful promise to Adam and Eve.

We read in the Bible about the promise God made. God promised that a woman would come, and she would have a Son. This Son of the woman would overcome Satan. Her Son would save us from sin.

The sin of Adam and Eve made them lose Heaven. But the great love and mercy of God promised them a Savior. A "savior" saves someone from harm. God promised Adam that He would send a Savior who would save men from the harm of sin. The Savior that God promised was God's own Son, Jesus.

God's Son would save mankind. This Savior would suffer for the sins of all men. Then God would open the gates of Heaven again.

1. A _____ saves someone from harm.

2. God promised to open the gates of _____.

3. The Savior would save men from _____.

4. The Savior would _____ for the sins of men.

God loves us very much. God is so good that He wants all of us to be with Him in Heaven.

After Adam and Eve sinned, God promised to send a Savior. God said that some day a special woman would have a Son. Her Son would make up to God for the sins of mankind. Her Son would accept the punishment that man deserves for his sins against God.

Adam and Eve were sorry for their sin. They never forgot the wonderful promise of God to send a Savior.

Adam and Eve had many children. They were all born with original sin on their souls. They taught their children about the promise of a Savior.

Adam and Eve knew that when they died, they would not go to Heaven and see God. God would send them to a place where they must wait until the Savior would come. Then God would open the gates of Heaven.

People who lived after Adam and Eve could not go to Heaven, because the gates of Heaven were closed until the Savior came. Only then would God open the gates of Heaven.

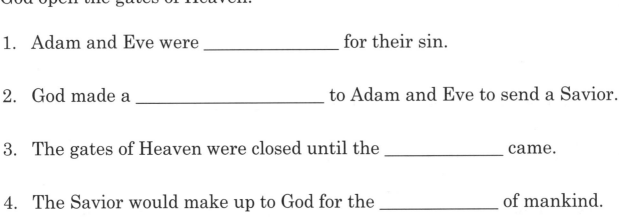

1. Adam and Eve were _____ for their sin.

2. God made a _____ to Adam and Eve to send a Savior.

3. The gates of Heaven were closed until the _____ came.

4. The Savior would make up to God for the _____ of mankind.

For many, many years people waited for the Savior. People prayed and prayed for the Savior to come. Holy men taught people to be good while waiting.

One holy man was Abraham. Abraham taught the people to love God. Moses was another holy man. Moses helped the people to obey God.

Finally, Jesus, the Son of God, the Savior, was born over 2,000 years ago. Jesus came into the world as a Baby, born in Bethlehem.

Jesus is the second Person of the Blessed Trinity. Jesus is the Son of God the Father, the first Person of the Blessed Trinity. Jesus is God made man.

Mary, the mother of Jesus, was very special because she had no original sin.

Jesus came to save all people on earth, so they could go to Heaven when they died. Jesus taught people how to be good. Jesus taught them how to obey the laws of God, His Father. Jesus taught people how much God loves them.

Jesus suffered and died on the cross for our sins and to open the gates of Heaven for us. When Jesus suffered and died on the cross, God the Father opened the gates of Heaven.

1. Jesus Christ is the Son of God made _____.

2. Jesus taught the people to _____ God's law.

3. Mary had no _____ sin.

4. Jesus taught people how much God _____ them.

23

God Promises a Savior: Review Questions

1. What wonderful promise did God make to Adam and Eve?
God promised that He would send a Savior to mankind.

2. What would the Savior do?
The Savior would save men from their sins. Then God would open the gates of Heaven again.

3. Who is the Savior God promised to mankind?
The Savior sent by God to save mankind is Jesus Christ. Jesus is the second Person of the Blessed Trinity, the Son of God the Father.

*4. When and where was Jesus born?
Jesus was born over 2,000 years ago, in a stable in Bethlehem.

*5. Is Jesus Christ both God and man?
Yes, Jesus Christ is both God and man.

*6. Who is the mother of Jesus?
The mother of Jesus is the Blessed Virgin Mary.

Moses and the Ten Commandments

The people on earth waited a long time for the Savior to come. While they were waiting, God spoke to a holy prophet named Moses. Moses was a great leader of the Jewish people. God told Moses He wanted the people to be good and to obey Him.

God gave Moses the Ten Commandments. These were ten commands, or laws, that God wants all people to obey.

We learn about the Ten Commandments in Exodus, the second book of the Bible. We read that God spoke to Moses on Mount Sinai. On this mountain God gave Moses the Ten Commandments.

The Bible says that the Ten Commandments were "written with the finger of God" on two stone tablets. God wrote them on stone so they could not be changed.

God told Moses to tell all the people about the Ten Commandments. God promised that if the people obeyed His Ten Commandments, He would bless them. He would give them and their children a long life, and keep them safe in the land He would give them.

1. God gave _____ the Ten Commandments.

2. The Commandments were written in stone to show they

    would never _____.

God gave Moses the Ten Commandments. The Ten Commandments are a guide to happiness. The Ten Commandments are signs of God's love for us.

If we obey the Ten Commandments which God gave us, we will be blessed in this life. And we will be able to go to Heaven. If we disobey the Ten Commandments of God, we will be unhappy, in this life and after we die.

If a watchmaker makes a watch, he knows how it is made. The watchmaker knows how the watch will run best. The watchmaker knows how to keep the watch running smoothly.

God made us. God is our Creator. He knows what is best for us. God knows how we can be happy because He made us.

God gave us the Ten Commandments so that we can be happy on earth. God gave us the Ten Commandments so that we can be happy with Him in Heaven.

1. The Ten Commandments are a guide to _____.

2. God is our _____, and knows what is best for us.

3. If we obey the Ten Commandments, we can be happy with God in _____.

4. God knows how we can be happy because He _____ us.

26

God gave us the Ten Commandments to show us the way to Heaven. God gave the Ten Commandments to all people.

We are commanded by God to obey His Ten Commandments. If we break a commandment, we are disobedient to God. Disobeying any of the Ten Commandments is a sin.

By obeying God's Ten Commandments, we show Him we love Him. If we obey God's Ten Commandments, we shall be happy on earth. If we obey God's Ten Commandments, we can go to Heaven.

The Commandments are God's laws for all people who ever lived. God's laws will never change. God gave Moses the Ten Commandments on stone tablets. By putting the Ten Commandments on stone, God shows us that they will never change.

When Jesus lived on the earth, He said, "If you love Me, keep My Commandments." Another time He said, "If you keep My Commandments, you shall live in My love."

One time a young man asked Jesus, "Master, what must I do to be saved?" Jesus answered, "Keep the Commandments."

1. Disobeying any one of the Ten Commandments is a _____.

2. By obeying the Commandments, we can go to _____.

3. "If you love Me, keep My _____."

4. God gave the Ten Commandments for all the _____ who ever lived.

27

Moses and the Ten Commandments: Review Questions

1. To whom did God give the Ten Commandments?
God gave the Ten Commandments to Moses.

2. Who was Moses?
Moses was a great prophet and leader of the Jewish people.

3. Who must obey the Ten Commandments?
Everyone must obey the Ten Commandments.

4. What do we show God when we obey His Commandments?
When we obey the Ten Commandments, we show God we love Him.

5. What can we expect if we obey the Ten Commandments?
If we obey the Ten Commandments, we will be happy on earth and with God in Heaven forever.

6. What can we expect if we disobey a Commandment of God?
If we disobey a Commandment of God, we will be very unhappy because we offended God, Who loves us.

7. What is disobeying a Commandment of God called?
Disobeying a Commandment of God is called a sin.

The First Three Commandments

The First Commandment of God is: **I am the Lord thy God; thou shalt not have strange gods before Me.**

The First Commandment tells us that we must worship only God. We must not worship anyone or anything but Him.

God is our Creator. We exist because God loves us and made us. Our first and main duty in life is to love and to obey God.

We must learn about God, love Him, and serve Him. We must adore Him, praise Him, and thank Him.

This First Commandment is the greatest commandment, Jesus said. In the Bible, in the Gospel of Saint Matthew, Jesus said, "Thou shalt love the Lord thy God with thy whole heart, and with thy whole soul, and with thy whole mind."

It is easy to love God because He is so good and loves us so! It is easy to love God Who has given us so much.

He gave us life, so we can be perfectly happy with Him in Heaven. He gives us our family. He gives us our mom and dad. He gives us our brothers and sisters, and our grandparents.

God gives us our Catholic Faith. He gives us the Catholic Church. He gives us priests. He gives us Himself in Holy Communion.

For all these gifts, we should worship, adore, and thank God. We should tell God often that we love Him.

1. The First Commandment tells us we must _____ only God.

2. The First Commandment is the _____ commandment.

The Second Commandment of God is: **Thou shalt not take the name of the Lord thy God in vain.**

We should use God's name with respect. God is our loving Father. God is our wonderful Creator. Without Him, we would not exist. So if we love God the way we should, we will use His name with respect.

The Bible says every knee will bend at Jesus' holy name. We should bow our heads whenever we say the name of Jesus.

The name of Jesus is so holy, that just by saying it, you are saying a prayer. Each time we say the name of Jesus with respect, we give Him joy and praise and glory.

St. Paul wrote in the Bible: "Whatever you do in word or work, do all in the name of the Lord Jesus Christ."

The name of Jesus is the shortest and the most powerful prayer. The apostles worked miracles in the name of Jesus.

The Second Commandment tells us we should use the name of God

with _____.

The Third Commandment of God is: **Remember thou keep holy the Lord's Day.**

God wants us to go to Mass on Sunday. It is the most important way to keep the Lord's Day holy. We should behave properly in church and say our prayers. We should follow the Mass prayers.

Our Lord Jesus is on the altar in the Sacrament of the Holy Eucharist. When we make our First Holy Communion, we will receive Jesus at Mass. We show God we love Him by going to Mass and receiving Holy Communion. We also obey the Third Commandment by keeping holy the Lord's Day in this way.

One of the prayers during Mass is "Holy, Holy, Holy, Lord God Almighty." This is a beautiful prayer we want to say during Mass.

God wants us to make Sunday a holy day in other ways. On Sundays, we must not do physical work that is not necessary. No one should do physical work on Sundays unless it is necessary.

God gave us Sunday as a day to rest, and do things we may not be able to do during the week. We can spend time with our families, study about God, visit the sick, or do other good deeds. If we truly keep holy the Lord's Day, we will become holy ourselves!

1. The Third Commandment tells us to keep the Lord's Day _____.

2. We make Sunday holy by going to _____, and by not doing physical work that is unnecessary.

3. God said Sunday should be a day of _____.

4. "Remember thou keep holy the _____ Day."

The First Three Commandments: Review Questions

1. What is the First Commandment of God?
The First Commandment of God is: "I am the Lord thy God; thou shalt not have strange gods before Me."

2. What does the First Commandment command us to do?
The First Commandment commands us to love and worship God. We must adore Him, praise Him, obey Him, and thank Him.

3. What is the Second Commandment of God?
The Second Commandment of God is: "Thou shall not take the name of the Lord thy God in vain."

4. What are we commanded by the Second Commandment of God?
By the Second Commandment of God we are commanded to use God's name with respect.

5. What is the Third Commandment of God?
The Third Commandment of God is: "Remember thou keep holy the Lord's Day."

6. What are we commanded by the Third Commandment?
By the Third Commandment we are commanded to worship God in a special way on Sunday, the Lord's Day, by assisting at Mass.

7. Are we commanded to keep Sunday holy in other ways?
Yes, we are commanded to keep Sunday holy by not doing unnecessary work.

8. Name some ways in which we would keep Sundays holy.
We would keep Sundays holy by spending time with our families, learning about God, spending more time in prayer, and doing good works.

First Quarter Review

God and Creation

We know from the Bible there is only one God. God never had a beginning, and God will always be. He is everywhere, knows all things, and can do all things. God is all-good, and all-loving.

We know there are three Persons in one God. There is God the Father, God the Son, and God the Holy Spirit. We call these three Persons in one God the Blessed Trinity.

We learn from the Bible that God is the Creator of all things. Long ago, He created the whole world out of nothing. God did not need the world. He created it because He is good, and wanted to share His goodness with us.

God created angels to share His love and goodness. He created them long before He created the world. Angels are pure spirits. They have a mind and a will, but they do not have bodies like ours.

God made the angels with very bright minds and free wills. He gave them great knowledge. But some of the angels did not want to obey God. They committed the first sin. Because of this, they could not stay in Heaven. The bad angels and their leader, Lucifer, were sent to Hell.

The good angels remained in Heaven, loving and adoring God. Some angels are messengers for God. Some angels are guardian angels. God gives each of us a guardian angel. Our guardian angels protect us, and help us to be good.

God also created man and woman to share in His love and goodness. God first created one man, Adam. God gave Adam a soul. The soul is the spiritual part of man. In the soul, man is made in the image and likeness of God. God gave man a body as well as a soul. God put Adam in Paradise. After some time passed, God made the woman, Eve, from a rib of Adam.

Adam and Eve are the parents of the human race. God filled their souls with divine grace. They were holy, happy, and intelligent. Their bodies would not die. They would go to Heaven without their bodies dying. Adam and Eve were very happy in Paradise.

The Fall of Man and the Promise of a Savior

Adam and Eve lived in the beautiful garden called Paradise. They were masters of the garden. God gave them only one command. They were not to eat of the tree of knowledge of good and evil. If they ate of the fruit of that tree, they would die. God commanded this so that Adam and Eve could show that they loved Him.

God allowed the bad angel, Satan, to appear as a serpent to Eve. Satan lied to Eve. Satan told Eve that if she would eat the forbidden fruit, she would become like God. Eve listened to Satan and ate the fruit. She then gave Adam some of the fruit, and he ate it too.

Adam and Eve disobeyed God, and committed the first sin on earth. We call this first sin "original sin."

As soon as Adam and Eve sinned, grace left their souls. They did not have great knowledge or perfect health any more. Their bodies would suffer and die. God sent them out of Paradise. He closed the gates of Heaven because no one can enter Heaven with sin on his soul.

Adam and Eve were the first parents of the entire human race. When they disobeyed God, they hurt all people born in all the years to come. All people are born with Adam and Eve's original sin. We are all born without God's grace. We are all born to suffering and hardship. Only one human person never had original sin: the Blessed Virgin Mary.

Even when God punished Adam and Eve, He still loved them. He promised them a Savior. The Savior would save men from sin. The Savior would open the gates of Heaven for all of us.

The Savior is God's own Son, Jesus. Jesus would suffer for the sins of all men. He would free us from original sin, and make it possible for us to go to Heaven.

For many, many years, people waited for the Savior. Finally, Jesus was born over 2,000 years ago, in a stable in Bethlehem. Jesus suffered and died on the Cross, so that the gates of Heaven would be opened for all of us.

The Ten Commandments

While the people on earth were waiting for the Savior to come, God spoke to a holy prophet and leader named Moses. God gave Moses His laws, the Ten Commandments. Through Moses, God gave the Ten Commandments to all people.

The Commandments are God's laws for men. God put the Ten Commandments on stone tablets. By putting them on stone tablets, God shows us that they will never change. If we do not follow a Commandment, we are disobedient to God. Disobeying any of the Ten Commandments is a sin.

God gave us the Ten Commandments to show us the way to Heaven. If we obey the Commandments, we shall be happy on earth, and we can go to Heaven. Once a young man asked Jesus, "Master, what must I do to be saved?" Jesus answered, "Keep the Commandments."

By obeying God's Ten Commandments, we show Him we love Him. When Jesus lived on earth, He said, "If you love Me, keep My Commandments." Another time Jesus said, "If you keep My Commandments, you shall live in My love."

The First Commandment of God is: **I am the Lord thy God; thou shalt not have strange gods before Me.** This first commandment tells us that we must worship only God. We must not worship anyone or anything but Him.

Jesus said that this First Commandment is the greatest commandment. In the Bible, Jesus tells us, "Thou shalt love the Lord thy God with thy whole heart, and with thy whole soul, and with thy whole mind."

The Second Commandment of God is: **Thou shalt not take the name of the Lord thy God in vain.** It tells us that we should use God's name with respect. God is our Creator. Without Him, we would not exist. If we love God the way we should, we will use His name with respect.

The Third Commandment of God is: **Remember thou keep holy the Lord's Day.** God gave us Sunday as a day to worship Him, and as a day to rest. We make Sunday holy by going to Mass and not doing any physical work that is not necessary.

WEEK NINE: Day 4

Review lessons from Weeks One through Nine.

WEEK NINE: Day 5

First Quarter Test.

Second Quarter

The Fourth Commandment

The Fourth Commandment of God is: **Honor thy father and thy mother.** The Fourth Commandment commands us to love, honor, and obey our parents. This commandment is repeated many times in the Bible.

Do you know what a debt is? It is something that one person owes to another.

The First Commandment commands us to honor God above everything else because He is our Creator. We owe a debt, we have a duty, to worship and respect our Creator.

In the same way, the Fourth Commandment commands us to honor our parents. They gave us life. We are alive because of God and because of our parents.

Our parents continue to keep us alive. They take care of us because they love us. They provide our food and clothing and a home for us.

Our parents love us very much. We want to love, honor, and obey our parents.

1. "Honor thy _____ and thy _____."

2. The Fourth Commandment commands us to _____,

   _____, and _____ our parents.

3. Our parents take care of us because they _____ us.

37

The Fourth Commandment of God is: "Honor thy father and thy mother."

In the Bible, we learn that Jesus "was subject" to His parents. This means that He obeyed His parents. Jesus obeyed their every command.

Jesus is God. He is the second Person of the Blessed Trinity. He wanted to show us how to obey the Commandments. Jesus obeyed His mother Mary and His foster father, Saint Joseph.

One time when Jesus was twelve years old, He went with Mary and Joseph to the big city of Jerusalem. They attended the religious services in the Temple. (The Temple was the place where the Jewish people worshipped God.) Later, Mary and Joseph found Jesus there teaching the priests about God. Mary asked Jesus to come home with them, and He came right away.

Being obedient to our parents means doing what they tell us right away. The Fourth Commandment commands us to be obedient, kind, and respectful to our parents.

1. Being _____ to our parents means doing what they tell us right away.

2. Jesus _____ His earthly parents.

The Fourth Commandment of God is: "Honor thy father and thy mother." We honor our parents when we are obedient, kind, and respectful to them. We must not argue with our parents or disrespectfully talk back to them. The Fourth Commandment requires that we honor and obey our parents.

God is especially pleased when children do good without being asked. Children should help their parents without being asked.

Saint Francis de Sales said one time, "Blessed are the obedient, for God will never allow them to go astray."

Saint Thérèse was very careful every day to be obedient to her father and her older sisters who took care of her after her mother died.

Jesus loves those who are obedient.

God gave each one of us the parents who are best for us. God wants us to show our love for Him by obeying the parents He gave us.

1. The Fourth Commandment requires that we _____ and_____ our parents.

2. Jesus loves those who are _____.

3. Saint Francis de Sales said, "Blessed are the _____."

The Fourth Commandment: Review Questions

*1. What is the Fourth Commandment of God?
The Fourth Commandment of God is: "Honor thy father and thy mother."

2. What are we commanded by the Fourth Commandment of God?
By the Fourth Commandment of God, we are commanded to obey our parents and to show them honor and respect.

3. Is it a sin for children to disobey their parents?
Yes, it is a sin for children to disobey their parents.

4. Must children love their parents?
Yes, it is a duty for children to love their parents.

5. Why should children honor and obey their parents?
Children should honor and obey their parents because their parents gave them life. God commands children to honor their parents.

The Fifth Commandment

The Fifth Commandment of God is: **Thou shalt not kill.** The Fifth Commandment means that we must not murder anyone. It also means that we must not harm anyone.

God is the Creator. God gives life, and God takes away life.

God made everyone. He made you and me. He made our parents. He made our brothers and sisters. He made everyone in our family, our grandparents, our uncles and aunts, our nephews and nieces.

He made the children in the neighborhood and their parents. He made all those who attend our church. Everyone God made is a child of God.

God is our Father in Heaven. God does not want us to murder anyone He made. He does not want us to harm anyone. That is why God gave us the Fifth Commandment.

The Fifth Commandment is "Thou shalt not _____."

41

The Fifth Commandment of God is: "Thou shalt not kill." God commands us not to commit murder. We must not murder anyone. Murder is a terrible sin.

The Fifth Commandment tells us to respect others. We break the Fifth Commandment if we hurt others on purpose. We break the Fifth Commandment if we fight with others.

If we hurt someone on purpose, such as fighting with someone, this is breaking the Fifth Commandment. If we hurt someone, such as kicking someone on purpose while playing, this is breaking the Fifth Commandment.

The Fifth Commandment teaches us to respect the bodies of others so they do not get hurt. It also commands us to respect our own bodies so we do not get hurt. We are not allowed to do dangerous things which might hurt our own bodies or the bodies of others.

1. The Fifth Commandment tells us to _____ others.

2. The Fifth Commandment tells us to _____ our own bodies.

The Fifth Commandment of God is: "Thou shalt not kill."

We are not allowed to murder anyone. No one may kill unborn babies. No one may kill babies or old people. No one may kill a sick person.

Jesus said in the Bible, "Love your neighbor as yourself." Who is our neighbor? Our neighbor is anyone at all whom we meet.

We are to treat our own brothers and sisters with special kindness. We are to be especially careful that we do not hurt anyone in our family. We are to be careful that we do not hurt our playmates.

The Fifth Commandment means we should take care of one another. We are commanded to care for one another.

The Fifth Commandment is important to think about every day. This Commandment reminds us to take care that we do not hurt anyone.

Our _____ is anyone at all whom we meet.

The Fifth Commandment: Review Questions

*1. What is the Fifth Commandment of God?
The Fifth Commandment of God is: "Thou shalt not kill."

2. What does the Fifth Commandment forbid?
The Fifth Commandment forbids us to murder anyone.

3. What are we commanded by the Fifth Commandment of God?
The Fifth Commandment of God commands us not to harm anyone.

4. What else does the Fifth Commandment command us to do?
The Fifth Commandment also commands us to respect the life of others.

5. Is it a sin against the Fifth Commandment of God to fight or hurt anyone on purpose?
Yes, it is a sin against the Fifth Commandment of God to fight or to hurt anyone on purpose.

The Sixth and Seventh Commandments

The Sixth Commandment of God is: **Thou shalt not commit adultery.** This commandment teaches us that we must keep our bodies and our behavior pure.

Most importantly, our souls must be kept clean. We must keep our bodies and our souls clean from sin. We must keep our bodies and our souls pure. The Sixth Commandment tells us to keep ourselves pure and clean.

Very often, things on television or the computer or in books can lead us to be unclean. It is best to stay away from the computer or those books or television programs. Then, it is easier to follow this commandment.

Mothers and fathers sometimes tell their children: "No, we cannot watch that program on television. It is a bad program." Sometimes parents say: "No, we cannot go to that movie, it is not clean." Children can keep pure and clean by obeying their parents.

Parents help children by teaching them how to obey the Commandments of God.

Our Lord Jesus said: "Blessed are the pure of heart, for they shall see God."

The Sixth Commandment tells us we must keep our bodies and our behavior _____.

45

The Seventh Commandment of God is: **Thou shalt not steal.** Stealing is taking what belongs to someone else without asking. It is a sin to steal.

This commandment tells us to respect what belongs to others. We must not take something that belongs to someone else. We must not break or damage what belongs to someone else.

If you own a toy, you expect others not to take it or break it. Others expect you not to take or break their things.

We must not steal.

It is against the Seventh Commandment. We must not take anything that is not ours. We must not take books or games that belong to someone else. We must not take dolls or balls that belong to a friend. We must not take Mom or Dad's things without asking.

We commit a sin against the Seventh Commandment if we take something without permission from the owner.

The Seventh Commandment tells us to respect what _____ to others.

The Seventh Commandment of God is : "Thou shalt not steal." We must not take or break what belongs to another.

This commandment also means we should be honest. If we cheat while playing games or doing our schoolwork, we are breaking the Seventh Commandment. If we take something from a store without paying for it, we break this commandment.

Sometimes, we borrow things and plan to give them back. These things might break or get lost. Even if this is an accident, we still must do something about it. We must pay for things we borrow and break. We must pay for things we borrow and lose.

It is stealing if we borrow something, break it, and do not pay for it.

1. The Seventh Commandment is "Thou shalt not _____."

2. The Seventh Commandment means we should be _____.

3. We must not _____ while playing games or doing our schoolwork.

4. If we break or lose something we borrowed, we must _____ for it.

47

The Sixth and Seventh Commandments: Review Questions

1. What is the Sixth Commandment of God?
The Sixth Commandment of God is: "Thou shalt not commit adultery."

2. What does the Sixth Commandment of God teach us?
The Sixth Commandment teaches us to be pure in our words, looks, and actions.

3. What is the Seventh Commandment of God?
The Seventh Commandment of God is: "Thou shalt not steal."

4. What does the Seventh Commandment of God tell us to do?
The Seventh Commandment of God tells us to respect what belongs to others.

5. What are sins against the Seventh Commandment of God?
Sins against the Seventh Commandment of God are stealing, breaking what belongs to someone else and not replacing it, cheating or being dishonest, and not returning things we have borrowed.

The Eighth Commandment

The Eighth Commandment of God is: "Thou shalt not bear false witness against thy neighbor." This Commandment commands us not to say things that are untrue when we are talking to other people.

We must always tell the truth. We must not lie. We must be honest.

Remember the devil and his lies to Eve? The devil is called the Father of Lies!

God our Father is in Heaven. He is the Father of Truth.

We obey the Eighth Commandment because we love our neighbors. Because we love them, we do not want to hide the truth from them. We also obey the Eighth Commandment because we love God, Who is the Truth. If God is the Truth, wouldn't we always want to share Him with others?

The Eighth Commandment tells us we must not _____.

The Eighth Commandment of God is: "Thou shalt not bear false witness against thy neighbor."

We are commanded by the Eighth Commandment to tell the truth about others. We must never say things about other people that are not true. Telling lies about someone can be worse than stealing his money.

We must not blame others for something we did.

We must not blame someone when we do not know for sure that they have done something wrong.

The Bible says "A good name is better than great riches."

We are commanded to tell the _____ about others.

The Eighth Commandment of God is: "Thou shalt not bear false witness against thy neighbor." We must always tell the truth. We must never tell a lie.

God has given us the gift of speech to tell the truth.

In Holy Communion, we receive Jesus on our tongues. We must not use our tongues to tell lies.

If we tell a lie, we must repair the harm. We must go back to the person and tell the truth. We must say we are sorry.

The Bible tells the story of Queen Esther. Queen Esther discovered a liar in her kingdom. Her uncle and many other people would die because of this lie. Queen Esther told the king about the lie. The king punished the liar.

St. Paul said to the people in Ephesus, "Put away lying and speak truth, each one with his neighbor, because we are members of one another." St. Paul meant that we are all children of God. We should speak the truth about everyone because each one of us is a child of God.

If we tell a lie, we must _____ the harm.

The Eighth Commandment: Review Questions

*1. What is the Eighth Commandment of God?
The Eighth Commandment of God is: "Thou shalt not bear false witness against thy neighbor."

2. What are we commanded by the Eighth Commandment?
We are commanded by the Eighth Commandment always to tell the truth.

3. Is it a sin to say false things about others?
It is a sin against the Eighth Commandment to say false things about others.

4. How valuable is a good name?
The Bible says, "A good name is better than great riches."

5. What are we commanded to do if we tell a lie?
If we tell a lie, we are commanded to repair the harm as far as we are able.

6. What did St. Paul say in the Bible about lying?
St. Paul said that we should "Put away lying and speak truth," because we are all children of God.

The Ninth and Tenth Commandments

The Ninth Commandment of God is: **Thou shalt not covet thy neighbor's wife.** This Commandment is for grown-ups. Grown-ups must not want to marry someone who is already married.

Jesus wants husbands to stay married to their own wives. Jesus wants wives to stay married to their own husbands. Other people should not try to take a wife from her husband, or a husband from his wife.

The Ninth Commandment tells us we must not want to marry someone

who is already _____.

The Tenth Commandment of God is: **Thou shalt not covet thy neighbor's goods.** This Commandment tells us we must not strongly desire to own what belongs to others.

Jesus wants us to be glad when other people have things. We should not be envious of other people because they have things we do not have. If a friend received a bicycle for his birthday, we should be glad for him. We should not want to take it away from him.

The Tenth Commandment forbids the sin of envy. If our brother received a football for Christmas, we should not be envious. We must be satisfied with what God gives us.

The Bible tells us to guard against the sin of envy.

"Take heed and guard yourself from all covetousness; for a man's life does not consist in the abundance of his possessions."

God judges us by our obedience to His commands. He does not judge us by what we own.

1. "Thou shalt not covet thy neighbor's _____."

2. The Tenth Commandment forbids the sin of _____.

The Tenth Commandment of God is: "Thou shalt not covet thy neighbor's goods."

The Tenth Commandment forbids being envious because someone has things we would like to own.

We should not be envious because a family is rich. We are to be glad because other people have nice things or gifts from God. We are to be glad with the things and gifts that God has given us.

We can work to obtain things for ourselves, however.

We can study hard to get a better grade. We can save our money to buy our own bicycle.

St. Paul wrote in the Bible: "Covetousness is the root of all evil."

"Some people," St. Paul wrote, "in their coveting have erred from the Faith, and have entangled themselves in many sorrows."

We are to be _____ with the things and gifts God has given us.

The Ninth and Tenth Commandments: Review Questions

1. What is the Ninth Commandment of God?
The Ninth Commandment of God is: "Thou shalt not covet thy neighbor's wife."

2. What is the Tenth Commandment of God?
The Tenth Commandment of God is: "Thou shalt not covet thy neighbor's goods."

3. What does the Tenth Commandment tell us to do?
The Tenth Commandment tells us to be glad when people have things or gifts from God.

4. What does the Tenth Commandment forbid?
The Tenth Commandment forbids the sin of envy. We must not strongly desire to have things that belong to others.

5. What does the Bible say about covetousness?
"Take heed and guard yourself from all covetousness; for a man's life does not consist in the abundance of his possessions."

6. What did St. Paul write about covetousness?
"Covetousness is the root of all evils. Some people, in their coveting have erred from the Faith, and have entangled themselves in many sorrows."

Mary, Our Blessed Mother

God made a promise to Adam and Eve to send a Savior. Once the Savior came, God would open the gates of Heaven.

After many years, God the Father sent His own Son, Jesus, our Savior, Who was born in Bethlehem over 2,000 years ago.

Jesus, the second Person of the Blessed Trinity, became Man. This is called the Incarnation. This is how it happened.

God the Father sent the Angel Gabriel to Mary. Mary was very holy. She never had original sin. Mary never committed any sin. She devoted her life to prayer.

The Angel Gabriel appeared to her. He said to her, "Hail, Mary, full of grace." Mary had no sin because she was filled with grace.

Then Saint Gabriel said, "Do not be afraid, Mary, for you shall have a Son. And you shall call Him Jesus."

1. The

   _____ means that Jesus became Man.

2. God the Father sent the Angel _____ to Mary.

57

The Angel Gabriel told Mary that she would have a Son, and His name was to be Jesus.

Mary asked how this could be, since she was not married. The angel said that the Holy Spirit would come upon her. And the "Holy One to be born shall be called the Son of God."

Mary immediately fell down on her knees. She said to Gabriel, and to God: "Behold! I am the handmaid of the Lord. Let it be done to me according to thy word." Thus, Mary agreed to be the Mother of God.

Mary said she was a servant of the Lord God. She would do whatever God asked of her. She would be obedient to His wishes or commands.

Mary loved God with all her heart. Mary wanted to be obedient immediately.

Mary was humble when she said she was a servant of the Lord.

Mary said to the Angel Gabriel: " Behold! I am the _____

of the Lord."

The Angel Gabriel was sent by God to Mary. He asked her to be the Mother of Jesus. We call this event the Annunciation. It was an announcement to the world that the long-awaited Savior was to be born.

Mary was very, very holy. She had no sin. Mary did not have original sin. This is called her Immaculate Conception. Her soul was perfectly clean from sin. Her soul was immaculate.

The Angel Gabriel told Mary that her cousin Elizabeth was going to have a baby. So Mary went to visit her cousin Elizabeth to help her.

Mary showed us by this that we must help people who need us. We call Mary's visit to Elizabeth the Visitation.

Elizabeth knew that Mary was chosen to be the Mother of God. Elizabeth knew that Mary's Baby was the Savior promised by God.

Elizabeth knelt down in front of Mary and said, "Blessed art thou among women, and blessed is the Fruit of thy womb."

1. The Angel Gabriel's visit to Mary is called the _____.

2. The Blessed Mother's visit to Elizabeth is called the _____.

Mary, Our Blessed Mother: Review Questions

1. Who is the Mother of Jesus?
The Mother of Jesus is the Blessed Virgin Mary.

2. What is the Incarnation?
The Incarnation is when Jesus, the Son of God, became Man.

3. What was the Annunciation?
The Annunciation was the announcing by the Angel Gabriel to Mary that she would be the Mother of the Son of God.

4. Was Mary free from original sin?
Yes, Mary, the Blessed Virgin Mother, was free from original sin.

5. What does the Immaculate Conception mean?
The Immaculate Conception means that Mary was without original sin from the first moment of her life.

6. What is the Visitation?
The Visitation is Mary's visit to her cousin Elizabeth.

Jesus, Our Savior

Of all the things that have happened since God created the world, the most important thing is that the Son of God became Man.

God sent His Beloved Son Jesus to be a Man in the world. Jesus came into the world to save mankind.

God chose Mary to be the mother of Jesus. God chose Joseph to be His foster father. Mary and Joseph were married in Nazareth. They were living in Nazareth when the Roman Emperor wanted to count all the people in the empire.

Though Mary was expecting Jesus to be born soon, they were forced to travel to Bethlehem. It was so crowded in Bethlehem that they could not find a room in the inn. They found space in a stable, which was kept warm by the animals.

Jesus, the Son of God, was born in a stable in Bethlehem.

The Bible says that Mary "wrapped Him in swaddling clothes and laid Him in a manger." A manger is a wooden container for hay from which animals eat.

Mary and Joseph knelt by the manger to adore little Baby Jesus.

1. The Son of God became a _____ in the world.

2. God sent His Beloved _____ into the world to save mankind.

3. Jesus was born in a _____ because there was no room

   for Joseph and Mary at the _____.

4. Mary laid Jesus in a _____.

Mary and Joseph adored Jesus in the stable in Bethlehem. At the same time, God sent an angel to shepherds in the nearby fields.

The shepherds were watching their flock of sheep. The Bible says "Behold, an angel of the Lord stood by them, and the glory of God shone round about them."

The angel said: "Do not be afraid, for behold, I bring you good news of great joy which shall be to all the people. For today, in the town of Bethlehem, a Savior has been born to you, Who is Christ the Lord.

"And this shall be a sign to you: you will find an Infant wrapped in swaddling clothes and lying in a manger."

Suddenly, there were thousands of angels. They were all praising God by singing: "Glory to God in the highest, and on earth peace to men of good will."

When the angels disappeared into Heaven, the shepherds said, "Let us go over to Bethlehem and see this thing that has come to pass which the Lord God has made known to us."

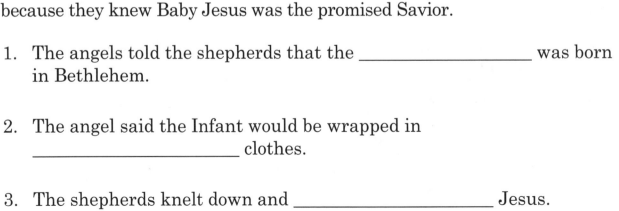

So they went with haste, and they found Mary and Joseph, and the Baby Jesus in swaddling clothes lying in a manger.

And they knelt down and adored Him because they knew Baby Jesus was the promised Savior.

1. The angels told the shepherds that the _____ was born in Bethlehem.

2. The angel said the Infant would be wrapped in _____ clothes.

3. The shepherds knelt down and _____ Jesus.

Besides the shepherds and the angels, a third group came to adore the Baby Jesus: the three Magi, or Wise Men, who lived in the East. The Magi were wise kings who studied the stars.

The Magi studied all the great writings of the prophets. They knew from the holy writings that a great King was to be born soon. When a special star appeared in the heavens, they knew this was the star to lead them to the King.

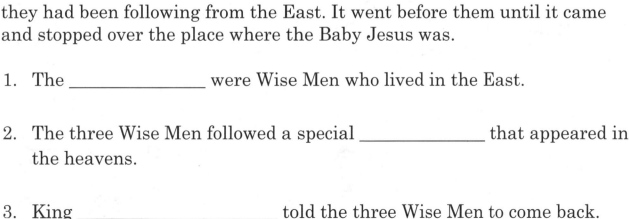

The three Magi first went to Jerusalem to King Herod. "Where is He that is born King of the Jews?" they asked. "We have seen His star in the East, and have come to worship Him."

King Herod asked the chief priests and teachers in Jerusalem where the Messiah was to be born. "Messiah" is one of the names the Jews used for the promised Savior.

"In Bethlehem," they said.

Then King Herod told the Magi to come back after they had found the Messiah in Bethlehem so that he could go and worship Him also, but we know that King Herod wanted only to harm the Baby Jesus.

After hearing King Herod's words, the Magi again beheld the star that they had been following from the East. It went before them until it came and stopped over the place where the Baby Jesus was.

1. The _____ were Wise Men who lived in the East.

2. The three Wise Men followed a special _____ that appeared in the heavens.

3. King _____ told the three Wise Men to come back.

Jesus, Our Savior: Review Questions

1. Where was Jesus born?
Jesus was born in a stable in Bethlehem, over 2,000 years ago.

2. What does the Bible say about Jesus in the stable?
The Bible says that Mary "wrapped Jesus in swaddling clothes and laid Him in a manger."

3. What was the good news of the angel to the shepherds?
The good news of the angel to the shepherds was that the Savior was born in Bethlehem.

4. What did the Magi, or three Wise Men, do?
The Magi, or three Wise Men, followed a special star to find the newborn King of the Jews.

The Holy Family

The three Wise Men from the East, called the Magi, found Jesus by following a special star. The star stopped over the place where Jesus was with His mother Mary and His foster father Joseph.

When the Magi saw Baby Jesus, they fell to their knees and worshiped Him. They knew He was a great king, the King of the Jewish people. They traveled from their faraway lands to do Him honor.

The Wise Men opened their treasures from the East and gave Him gifts. They gave Baby Jesus gifts of gold, frankincense, and myrrh.

In the night, an angel warned the Magi not to return to Jerusalem because King Herod wanted to kill the Baby Jesus. They went back to their own countries in the East by another way.

The Magi did not return

to Jerusalem because they

knew _____ wanted to kill the Baby Jesus.

After the three Wise Men, or Magi, left the Holy Family, an angel appeared to Saint Joseph while he was sleeping. The Bible says that the angel said to Joseph, "Arise, and take the Child and His mother, and flee into Egypt, and remain there until I tell thee. For King Herod will seek the Child to destroy Him."

Joseph immediately arose and took Baby Jesus and His mother Mary away in the middle of the night. Joseph quietly led the little donkey carrying Mary and Baby Jesus. Moving rapidly, they escaped into the country of Egypt.

King Herod realized that he had been tricked by the Magi. King Herod became very angry because the Magi did not return to tell him where the Baby Jesus was living.

Herod was so angry that he did one of the most terrible things that ever happened in human history. King Herod sent his soldiers to Bethlehem to kill all the little boys who were two years old or younger!

Herod was very, very evil, and his soldiers were very, very cruel.

All the parents in Bethlehem were weeping and moaning for the dead babies. The Bible says there was "loud lamentation" for the children who were no more.

Today, we call these little babies who were killed the Holy Innocents.

1. Herod sent his soldiers to kill all baby boys in Bethlehem younger than

    _____ years old.

2. We call these little babies the _____ _____.

Jesus, Mary, and Joseph lived in Egypt until the evil King Herod died. When Herod was dead, an angel of the Lord appeared to Joseph. The angel told Joseph it was safe to return to their home.

"Arise, and take the Child and His mother, and go into the land of Israel," said the angel. So Joseph immediately obeyed. He arose and took the Holy Family and went and settled in their home town. They settled in Nazareth.

They lived a life of prayer and good works for the poor. Joseph was a carpenter and taught Jesus how to build furniture.

Every year, the Holy Family went to Jerusalem for a special time of prayer. Every year, they would go to pray at the Temple in Jerusalem.

Once when they were in Jerusalem, when Jesus was twelve years old, Mary and Joseph could not find Jesus. They looked for Him for three days. Finally, they found the Boy Jesus in the Temple, teaching the elders and answering questions for the priests and teachers.

Jesus told Mary and Joseph that He must be doing work for His Father in Heaven.

Mary and Joseph asked that He come back home with them. Jesus went back to Nazareth with them immediately. Jesus was always obedient to them. He obeyed them immediately.

Jesus stayed in Nazareth with Mary and Joseph for many years.

1. When the Holy Family left Egypt, they went to live in

   _____.

2. When Jesus was twelve, He answered questions for the

   _____ and teachers.

3. Jesus _____ His parents immediately.

67

The Holy Family: Review Questions

1. What did the Magi give Jesus?
The Magi gave Jesus gifts of gold, frankincense, and myrrh.

2. Why did Joseph take Mary and Baby Jesus to Egypt?
Joseph took Mary and Baby Jesus to Egypt because an angel warned
Joseph that King Herod wanted to kill Jesus.

3. What terrible thing did King Herod do?
The terrible thing that King Herod did was to order his soldiers to kill
all the little boy babies in Bethlehem who were two years old or younger.

4. What do we call the little babies who were killed by King Herod?
We call the little babies who were killed by King Herod the Holy Innocents.

5. Where did the Holy Family live after they returned from Egypt?
The Holy Family lived in Nazareth after they returned from Egypt.

Second Quarter Review

The Fourth, Fifth, Sixth and Seventh Commandments

The Fourth Commandment of God is: **Honor thy father and thy mother.** The Fourth Commandment commands us to love, honor, and obey our parents. This Commandment is repeated many times in the Bible.

In the Bible, we learn that Jesus was "subject" to His parents. This means that He obeyed His parents. Jesus obeyed their every request.

Jesus is God. He is the second Person of the Blessed Trinity. He wanted to show us how to obey the Commandments. So He obeyed His earthly parents, Mary and Joseph.

The Fifth Commandment of God is: **Thou shalt not kill.** The Fifth Commandment means that we must not murder anyone.

God is the Creator. God gives life, and God takes away life. Only God may decide when it is time for a person to die.

The Fifth Commandment tells us to respect others. We break the Fifth Commandment if we hurt others on purpose. We break the Fifth Commandment if we fight with others.

The Fifth Commandment teaches us to respect the bodies of others so they don't get hurt. It also commands us to respect our own bodies so we don't get hurt. The Fifth Commandment teaches us to care for one another.

The Sixth Commandment of God is: **Thou shalt not commit adultery.** It teaches us that we must always keep our words, looks, and actions pure. Our Lord Jesus once said: "Blessed are the pure of heart, for they shall see God."

The Seventh Commandment of God is: **Thou shalt not steal.** Stealing is taking what belongs to someone else without asking. Stealing is borrowing something, and not replacing it if we break it. The Seventh Commandment teaches us to respect the things of others.

The Seventh Commandment also teaches us to be honest. If we cheat while playing games or doing our schoolwork, we are breaking the Seventh Commandment.

The Eighth, Ninth, and Tenth Commandments

The Eighth Commandment of God is: **Thou shalt not bear false witness against thy neighbor.** This Commandment commands us not to say things that are untrue.

We are commanded by the Eighth Commandment to tell the truth about others. We must not say things about other people that are not true. We must not blame others for something we did. We do not blame someone when we do not know for sure that they have done something wrong.

We obey the Eighth Commandment because we love our neighbors. Because we love them, we do not want to hide the truth from them. We also obey the Eighth Commandment because we love God, Who is the Truth. If God is the Truth, wouldn't we always want to share Him with others?

The Ninth Commandment of God is: **Thou shalt not covet thy neighbor's wife.** Although this Commandment is for grown-ups, it commands us all that we must be pure in our thoughts and desires. Grown-ups must not want to marry someone who is already married.

The Tenth Commandment of God is: **Thou shalt not covet thy neighbor's goods.** This Commandment tells us we must not strongly desire to own what belongs to others.

Jesus wants us to be glad when other people have things. We should not be envious of other people because they have things we do not have. The Tenth Commandment forbids the sin of envy.

The Coming of the Savior

Over 2,000 years ago, the Son of God, the second Person of the Blessed Trinity, became Man. This is called the Incarnation.

God the Father sent the Angel Gabriel to Mary, to ask her to be the mother of His Son. Mary was very holy. She never had original sin. For this reason, the angel greeted her with the words "Hail Mary, full of grace." Mary was filled with grace because she had no sin.

When the angel asked Mary to be the mother of Jesus, she answered that she was a servant of the Lord. She would do whatever God asked of her. This event is called the Annunciation.

Mary was married to a holy man named Joseph. God chose Joseph to be the foster father of Jesus on earth. When it was time for Jesus to be born, Joseph and Mary had to travel to Bethlehem. When they arrived, there was no room for them at the inn. They found a place to stay in a stable.

Jesus, the Son of God, was born in a stable in Bethlehem. Mary wrapped Him in swaddling clothes, and laid Him in a manger. When Jesus was born, God sent angels to the shepherds, to tell them of the Savior's birth. The shepherds came to worship the Savior with great joy.

Wise Men, or Magi, from the East also came to worship the Baby Jesus. They were led to the stable by a star that appeared in the sky. They brought treasures to give to the newborn King.

King Herod did not want to worship the Savior. He was afraid of the new King, and wanted to kill Him. God warned Joseph in a dream, and the Holy Family escaped to Egypt. The wicked King Herod tried to find the Baby King. He sent his soldiers to Bethlehem to kill all the baby boys two years old or younger. Today, we call the little boys who were killed instead of Jesus the Holy Innocents.

The Holy Family lived in Egypt until King Herod died. When they returned, they went to Nazareth. There the Child Jesus lived until He grew to be a Man. In all things, He was obedient to His parents.

Please review the lessons.

Second Quarter Test.

Third Quarter

Jesus Is God

God is all-good, all-loving, all-knowing, and all-powerful. God is everywhere and He can do all things. There is no end to God's greatness.

There is no end to the greatness of Jesus because He is God. Jesus did many wonderful things that showed the world that He is God.

Jesus is God the Son, the second Person of the Blessed Trinity. He came down from Heaven and became Man. He did this to open Heaven for us.

Jesus chose a very special woman, Mary, to be His Mother. Only a very special woman, free from original sin, could be the Mother of God. Jesus chose holy Saint Joseph to be His foster father on earth. Jesus knew He needed a very holy man to protect His Holy Family.

1. Jesus showed the world that He is _____.

2. Only a woman free from _____ _____ could be the Mother of God.

73

Jesus is God the Son, the second Person of the Blessed Trinity. Jesus came down from Heaven to open the gates of Heaven for us. Jesus taught us about Himself and His Father and the Holy Spirit.

Jesus did many wonderful things while He lived on earth. The Bible tells about many of the things that showed Jesus is God.

Our Lord worked many miracles. We know only God can work miracles. Jesus cured sick people who were ill for many years. Jesus gave sight to the blind and made the lame walk. He turned water into wine.

Jesus fed thousands of people with just a little bit of food. He walked on water and quieted raging storms. Jesus brought dead people back to life.

Jesus knew what people were thinking. He could read their hearts. Jesus forgave people their sins. This shows that He was God. Only God can forgive sins.

You or I could not do any of these things. Why was Jesus able to do such things? Because nothing is impossible with God!

1. Jesus is the _____ Person of the Blessed Trinity.

2. Jesus _____ sick people.

3. Only _____ can work miracles. Only _____ can forgive sins.

4. Jesus showed us He is God by working _____ and _____ sins.

74

A poor man sat each day by the Temple gates and begged. He was unable to work because he was born blind. One day, Jesus walked close by the blind man.

The blind man heard that Jesus was near. "Jesus," he shouted, "Help me!"

Jesus looked at him with love. He would help. Jesus put clay on the blind man's eyes. He told the blind man to wash his eyes.

The blind man obeyed Jesus. As soon as he did so, the blind man could see.

Jesus cured the man born blind! Gratefully, the blind man ran to Our Lord to thank Him.

One day, a sad group of people passed Jesus. Men were carrying a boy who had died. The boy's mother was crying. He was her only son.

Jesus told the mother, "Do not cry." He touched the dead boy and said, "Young man, arise!" The boy opened his eyes. He was alive! The boy's mother was so happy now. Jesus had given her back her good son!

Jesus worked these miracles because He loves each one of us. Jesus worked these miracles because He is God.

1. Jesus made the blind man _____ and brought the dead boy back to _____.

2. Jesus worked miracles because He _____ each one of us.

Jesus Is God: Review Questions

*1. Did one of the Persons of the Blessed Trinity become Man?
Yes, the second Person, the Son of God, became Man.

*2. What is the name of the Son of God made Man?
The name of the Son of God made Man is Jesus Christ.

*3. Who is the Mother of Jesus?
The Mother of Jesus is the Blessed Virgin Mary.

4. What was special about Mary that allowed her to be the Mother of God?
Mary was free from original sin, and she never committed any sin.

5. Why did Jesus work miracles?
Jesus worked miracles to show us He is God, and because He loves each one of us.

6. What are two of the miracles that Jesus worked?
Jesus made the blind man see and brought the dead boy back to life.

Jesus Is Man

Jesus, the second Person of the Blessed Trinity, came down from Heaven to save us. He came to reopen the gates of Heaven for us.

Jesus, the Son of God, took a body and soul like ours. He became human like us. Mary and Joseph took care of Him. He was given the name Jesus, as the Angel Gabriel had said.

Jesus is God but He is also Man because He has a body and soul. Jesus Christ is God made Man. Jesus is all-good, all-knowing, and all-powerful because He is God.

Jesus Christ has a human nature. Jesus felt joy and happiness, just as we do. He enjoyed friends. He loved His mother's company. He loved to be with little children. Jesus helped His foster father in the carpenter shop.

Jesus felt hunger and thirst, cold and heat. He felt tired and sleepy. Jesus felt sadness and pain. Jesus felt the things that you and I feel because He has a body and soul like ours. Jesus is like us in everything except sin.

Jesus is only one Person. But He is both God and Man.

1. In His human nature, Jesus has a _____ and

   _____ .

2. Jesus is both _____ and _____, but He is only one Person.

3. Jesus is like us in everything except _____ .

Jesus was not only Man: He was a perfect Man, the only perfect Man. His Body was formed in the womb of His most holy and pure Mother. It was formed miraculously through the power of the Holy Spirit.

Jesus was free from all sin because He is God the Son. He gave us the example of how to act. Jesus knew what it meant to be poor and to work hard. He knew what it meant to be disliked and falsely accused. Jesus knew what it meant to be betrayed by the closest of friends.

Jesus did not need to suffer any of these things, but He wanted to suffer these things in order to be close to us.

When we think of these things, we see that Jesus understands our own sufferings. We can never say that Jesus does not understand our sufferings.

Jesus wants us to go to Him with what hurts us and join our own pains to His. If I go to Jesus each time I have a problem, then I am truly a child of God.

1. Jesus was like us in all things except that He was free from all

   _____.

2. Jesus knew what it meant to be _____ and to

   _____ hard.

3. Jesus understands our _____.

4. Each time I have a problem, I should go to _____.

Jesus, the Son of God, became one of us so that He could teach us important things. He taught us how to treat each other. He said, "Love one another." Jesus taught us how we should live. If we listen to what Jesus taught us, then we will know how to love God.

Jesus became one of us so that He could teach us about God, His Father. Jesus taught us how we should pray. When we pray, we are talking to God.

God wants us to talk to Him often. He wants us to be close to Him. That is what the Bible means when we read, "Pray without ceasing."

We should talk to Jesus about our family. We should talk to Him about our home schooling. We should ask Jesus to give us all the help we need to be saints. We should ask Jesus to bless all the people we see and meet each day.

We should think of God the Father when we see the beautiful world He has created. We should remember to thank Him for all the good things He has given us. We should remember how great God is and glorify Him, because that is the most important reason to pray.

When we have done something wrong, we should tell Jesus we are sorry and ask His forgiveness.

When we tell Jesus things, we should listen quietly for His answer. Jesus will not say words in our ears, but He will put thoughts in our minds.

Jesus became one of us because He wants us to know Him. If we know Jesus, we will love Him and want to serve Him. If we do these things, then one day we will be happy with Him in Heaven!

1. Jesus said, "Love _____ _____."

2. We should _____ God for all the good things He has given us.

3. If we know Jesus, we will _____ Him.

Jesus Is Man: Review Questions

1. Why did Jesus, the second Person of the Blessed Trinity, become Man?
Jesus, the second Person of the Blessed Trinity, became Man to open the gates of Heaven for us.

2. Is Jesus Christ both God and Man?
Yes, Jesus Christ is both God and Man.

3. What did Jesus come to teach us?
Jesus came to teach us how to treat each other and how to love God.

4. What is prayer?
Prayer is talking to God.

Jesus Suffered and Died

Jesus lived with His Holy Family for thirty years. In all things, Jesus quickly and lovingly obeyed Mary and Joseph.

When Jesus was thirty years old, He left His loving home in Nazareth. Then it was time to begin His mission to the world.

Jesus taught many things and worked many miracles. He came down from Heaven to suffer and die for our sins. He came to reopen the gates of Heaven for us.

Jesus suffered and died for the sins of our first parents and for our sins. That was His Father's will and Jesus obeyed. He suffered for all the sins that would ever be committed. He did this to open the gates of Heaven for us once again.

Jesus loves us so much that He suffered and died rather than see us shut out of Heaven. It is sin that keeps us out of Heaven.

Sin causes Jesus much suffering and pain, and sin makes us enemies of God. We must stay very far away from sin. If we remember what our sins have done to Jesus, it will be easier to stay away from sin.

Like Jesus, we must always do the will of our Father in Heaven.

1. Jesus was _____ years old when He began His mission to the world.

2. Jesus suffered for our _____, so that we could go to Heaven. It is sin that keeps us out of Heaven.

3. We must always do the _____ of our Father in Heaven.

After the Last Supper, Jesus took His apostles into the garden to pray. Jesus knew He soon would be arrested. Jesus knew He soon would be beaten and nailed to the cross.

Jesus saw all the sins of the world. Jesus saw the sinners who would be sorry. Jesus saw the people who would not be sorry for their sins.

Poor Jesus suffered so much in the garden that first Holy Thursday night! Knowing what was to happen caused a sweat of blood all over His Body. Jesus prayed to His Heavenly Father, "Father, not My Will, but Thine be done!"

Out of love for us, Jesus let the soldiers arrest Him. How much He suffered for us! His own apostle, Judas, betrayed Him for thirty pieces of silver. The other apostles ran away and left Jesus alone with His enemies.

His enemies brought Jesus before the Jewish rulers and told lies about Him. Jesus, Who never committed sin, was thrown into prison. The soldiers spat upon Him and beat Him and whipped Him. They made cruel fun of Him and called Him bad names. They mocked Him and placed a crown of thorns upon His Sacred Head.

Jesus suffered all this and much more because He loves us.

1. After the _____ _____, Jesus went with His apostles to pray.

2. The soldiers placed a crown of _____ on His Sacred Head.

3. Jesus suffered so much because He _____ us.

For our sins, Jesus carried His heavy Cross to Mount Calvary. Weak from the beatings, He fell three times under the weight of the cross. On the way, Jesus met His sorrowful Mother. How Mary must have suffered when she saw her Son!

At last, Jesus reached the top of Mount Calvary. The soldiers nailed His hands and feet to the Cross. For three hours, Jesus suffered terribly on the Cross. Drop by drop, His Precious Blood fell upon the ground.

Surrounded by His enemies, Jesus slowly began to die. Only His holy Mother Mary, St. Mary Magdalen, and His apostle St. John stayed at the foot of the Cross.

Jesus looked up to Heaven and said, "Father, forgive them, for they know not what they do."

On that first Good Friday, Jesus died to make up for our sins.

Dear Jesus, forgive me. I am sorry for having offended Thee.

1. On _____ _____, Jesus died to make up for our sins.

2. Jesus suffered on the Cross for _____ hours.

3. The apostle Saint _____ stayed at the foot of the Cross.

4. Jesus died on Mount _____.

5. Dear Jesus, I am _____ for having offended Thee.

Jesus Suffered and Died: Review Questions

1. How old was Jesus Christ when He began His mission to the world?
Jesus Christ was thirty years old when He began His mission to the world.

2. Why did Jesus become Man?
Jesus became Man to teach us and to open the gates of Heaven for us.

3. What keeps us out of Heaven?
Sin keeps us out of Heaven.

*4. How did Jesus satisfy for the sins of all men?
Jesus satisfied for the sins of all men by His sufferings and death on the Cross.

5. When and where did Jesus die?
Jesus died on Good Friday, on Mount Calvary.

Jesus Rose from the Dead

After Jesus died, His Body was placed in a tomb. The enemies of Jesus remembered His words before He died: "After three days, I will rise again." A large, heavy stone was rolled before the entrance of the tomb. Soldiers were placed outside to guard the tomb.

Jesus was dead, but He had won back the holy life of grace for us. We were given back the right to be called children of God. We were given back the gift of being able to live forever in Heaven.

After His death, Our Lord's Soul went to a place where the souls of the good people went before Jesus reopened the gates of Heaven. How happy they were to see Him! How long they had waited!

The third day after Jesus died, a wondrous thing took place. The earth quaked! The heavy stone rolled away! A blinding light came out of the tomb! The soldiers were knocked to the ground!

"Jesus Christ, the Son of God, has risen!"

"Jesus Christ, the second Person of the Blessed Trinity, has risen!"

"Jesus Christ Our Lord, True God and True Man, has risen from the dead!"

1. Jesus said, "After three days, I will _____ again."

2. After He died, Our Lord's soul went to a place where the souls of the

   _____ people went.

3. Jesus Christ has _____ from the dead!

Three women went to the tomb of Jesus on Easter Sunday morning. They wanted to anoint the body of Jesus. They wondered who would roll back the large stone for them. They did not know an angel had rolled back the heavy stone.

When they came to His tomb, they saw things were changed. The soldiers were gone and the entrance was clear—the stone rolled back! The women entered the tomb and found it empty.

Right away, they thought the enemies of Jesus must have stolen His Body. Suddenly, they saw an angel dressed in white. He said, "Why do you look for Jesus? He is not here. He is risen!"

Mary Magdalen, one of the women, went out of the tomb and saw someone walking in the garden. She ran to Him and said: "Please, Sir, tell me where they have taken Him."

The Man asked, "Why are you crying, Mary?" She knew His voice! She looked up joyfully and cried, "Master!"

It was Jesus!

Jesus did not have the bruised, beaten, bloody Body of Good Friday, three days before. His risen, immortal Body now was beautiful and glorious!

Mary ran to tell the apostles what she had seen. "Jesus is alive! He is risen as He said!"

Peter and John ran out to the tomb. They looked inside and it was empty. They believed. Truly He had risen from the dead!

1. On Easter Sunday, the stone was rolled away and the tomb of Christ was empty because Jesus had _____.

2. Jesus' risen Body was _____ and _____.

Jesus still had many things to teach His apostles. He ate and drank with them. His glorified Body appeared and disappeared at will. He passed through solid walls and doors. He worked more miracles.

Jesus gave His apostles the power to forgive sins. He told them, "Whose sins you shall forgive, they are forgiven. Whose sins you shall retain, they are retained."

One day, Jesus asked Peter three times, "Do you love Me?"

"Yes, Lord," Peter answered, "You know all things. You know I love You."

Then Jesus told Peter, "Feed My lambs. Feed My sheep."

Do you know that we are His lambs? Our Good Shepherd, Jesus, told Peter, the first pope, that the Catholic Church must protect us and guide us to Heaven.

Our Lord told His apostles, "Go to all nations. Baptize them in the name of the Father, and of the Son, and of the Holy Spirit."

Forty days after His Resurrection, the time had come for Our Lord to leave His apostles. From a mountaintop, 120 of our Lord's friends watched Him ascend from the ground. As they watched Him rising higher and higher into the clouds, two angels appeared and spoke. The angels promised, "Jesus will return one day in the same way you have watched Him leave."

By His Death, Resurrection, and Ascension, Jesus won back for us the life of grace lost by Adam's sin. Jesus opened the gates of Heaven once more!

1. Our Lord told His apostles to go to all nations and _____ them.

2. Jesus ascended into Heaven _____ days after He rose from the dead.

Jesus Rose from the Dead: Review Questions

1. What happened on the third day after the death of Jesus?
Jesus Christ rose from the dead the third day after His death.

2. What do we call Our Lord's rising from the dead?
We call Our Lord's rising from the dead the Resurrection.

3. How many days did Jesus stay with the apostles and disciples before ascending into Heaven?
Jesus stayed with the apostles and disciples for forty days before ascending into Heaven.

4. What did Jesus tell St. Peter? What does this mean?
Jesus told St. Peter to "Feed My lambs. Feed My sheep." This means that the Catholic Church must protect us and guide us to Heaven.

5. What did Jesus tell the apostles?
Jesus told the apostles to go out and baptize all nations in the name of the Father, and of the Son, and of the Holy Spirit.

The Catholic Church

Before Jesus ascended into Heaven, He gave instructions to His apostles. Jesus told them not to leave the city until the Holy Spirit came. Jesus promised that the Holy Spirit would come and teach them.

The apostles and Our Lord's Blessed Mother returned to the Upper Room. This was the place where Our Lord had His Last Supper. The apostles stayed in the Upper Room because they were frightened of Our Lord's enemies.

All the windows and doors were securely locked. The apostles and the Blessed Mother prayed and fasted for nine days. On the tenth day, what do you think happened? A mighty gust of wind blew through the whole house! Tongues of fire appeared in the air and hung over the heads of every person in the room!

The Holy Spirit, the Spirit of Truth, had come!

A sudden change came over each one in the room. Peter, no longer frightened, boldly ran outside on the balcony to tell the crowd in the streets below all about Jesus. People from many different countries were visiting Jerusalem on that feast day.

The Holy Spirit worked another miracle! Many people heard St. Peter speak in their own languages! After Peter finished speaking, three thousand men, as well as many more women and children, asked to be baptized.

This special day is called Pentecost Sunday. Pentecost is the birthday of the Catholic Church. The Holy Spirit speaks to all of us today through the Catholic Church.

1. The birthday of the Church is _____ _____.

2. The Holy Spirit speaks to all of us today through the _____ _____.

At the Last Supper, Our Lord made the apostles bishops. They were the first bishops of the Catholic Church.

Peter was called Simon at first, but Jesus changed his name. Jesus said to him, "You are Peter, and upon this Rock I will build My Church." Peter means rock. Jesus said this to show that His Church on earth has a firm foundation, like a rock.

Jesus made Saint Peter the head of Our Lord's Church on earth. Saint Peter was the first Pope. The Pope is the head of the Catholic Church on earth.

All of our bishops and priests today trace their priesthood back to the apostles. All the Popes are descended from Saint Peter, the first pope.

The Pope rules Christ's Church on earth. The Pope guides us all. The bishops help the Pope care for us all. Priests help the bishops take care of us all.

The Pope, the bishops, the priests, and all baptized Catholics form the Church that Jesus Christ started.

Jesus knew that a Church was needed to carry out the work that He began. The Catholic Church was started by Our Lord Jesus Christ. It is the only Church that Jesus started. It is the one true Church. It is the only true Church because it is the only Church Jesus started.

Our Lord Jesus Christ is always with us because He lives in His Catholic Church.

1. The _____ is the head of the Catholic Church.

2. Our Lord made the apostles _____.

3. Jesus made St. Peter our first _____.

Jesus wants to give us every help we need to get to Heaven. That is why He started the Catholic Church. Jesus promised us that the Church would last until the end of the world.

The Church teaches all people at all times. The Church is in all countries of the world. The Catholic Church teaches us God's Truths.

Jesus sent God the Holy Spirit to protect His Church. God the Holy Spirit, through the Catholic Church, teaches us God's truth. The Holy Spirit, through the Catholic Church, helps us to be good.

God gives us all the help we need to save our souls.

That special help is called grace. We gain grace through the sacraments of the Catholic Church. Grace is God's life within us. We need grace to get to Heaven.

Jesus Christ started the Catholic Church because He wants to help everyone to go to Heaven.

1. Jesus started the _____ Church.

2. The Catholic Church will last until the end of the _____.

3. _____ is God's life within us.

4. The Catholic Church teaches us God's _____.

5. We gain grace through the _____ of the Catholic Church.

1. **What is the birthday of the Catholic Church?**
   The birthday of the Catholic Church is Pentecost, when God the Holy Spirit descended upon the apostles and Our Blessed Mother.

2. **What is the only Church started by Our Lord Jesus Christ?**
   The Catholic Church is the only Church started by Jesus Christ.

3. **Who is the head of the Catholic Church? Who was the first head of the Catholic Church?**
   The Pope is the head of the Catholic Church. St. Peter was the first Pope.

4. **What is grace?**
   Grace is the life of God in our soul. It is a special help we obtain through the sacraments.

5. **Why did Our Lord Jesus Christ start the Catholic Church?**
   Our Lord Jesus started the Catholic Church to help us get to Heaven.

6. **Whom did Our Lord Jesus Christ send to protect the Catholic Church?**
   Our Lord Jesus Christ sent God the Holy Spirit, the third Person of the Blessed Trinity, to protect the Catholic Church.

The Seven Sacraments and Grace

All grace comes to us from Our Lord Jesus Christ, the second Person of the Blessed Trinity. Jesus sends us all His grace through the Catholic Church.

The two most important ways to gain grace are through prayer and the sacraments.

If we pray or do what is right, God sends us grace. This kind of grace is called actual grace. Actual grace helps us to be good. Actual grace enlightens our mind and strengthens our will to do good and to avoid evil.

There is another kind of grace called sanctifying grace. Adam and Eve had sanctifying grace before they committed sin. Sanctifying grace gives our souls a new life. Sanctifying grace makes us holy.

When we receive a sacrament worthily, God sends us sanctifying grace. Our Lord Jesus gave His Church seven sacraments to help us gain sanctifying grace.

These seven sacraments are very special and holy gifts from God. Sacraments make our souls holy and pleasing to God.

Sacraments give us a share in God's life of grace.

Sacraments make us children of God and temples of the Holy Spirit. Sacraments will help us get to Heaven.

1. _____ grace helps us to be good.

2. _____ grace gives our souls new life.

The Catholic Church teaches us that "a sacrament is an outward sign instituted by Christ to give grace." Let's see what that means.

"Instituted" means "started." The Sacraments were started by Jesus Himself, the second Person of the Blessed Trinity.

A sacrament is an "outward sign" of grace being given to a person. This means we can see the sacrament being given. We can see the water in the sacrament of Baptism, for example. We can hear the words as the sacrament is being given.

We cannot see grace but we can see the sign of the sacrament which gives grace.

All sacraments were instituted by Our Lord Jesus Christ. All of the seven sacraments were given to us by Jesus. Jesus gave us sacraments to give us grace, His life in our souls. When we receive a sacrament, Our Lord Jesus Christ sends God the Holy Spirit to pour grace into our souls.

If we receive the sacraments in the right way, we will gain many blessings from God. When we receive a sacrament, it is really Our Lord Jesus Christ Who gives the sacrament to us through a priest or bishop.

1. A _____ is an outward sign instituted by Christ to give

    _____.

2. When we receive a sacrament, it is _____ Who gives it to us through a priest or bishop.

There are two kinds of grace. The two kinds of grace are sanctifying grace and actual grace.

Sanctifying grace makes us holy. We receive sanctifying grace whenever we receive a sacrament worthily.

Actual grace helps us to be good. We receive actual grace when we pray and when we do good deeds.

If we are annoyed with our baby brother, Our Lord Jesus Christ will send us the grace to be patient and kind. If we break a dish, Our Lord Jesus Christ will give us the grace to tell our mother and father the truth.

Jesus sends us actual grace to help us stay away from sin. When we ask Him, Jesus will always give us the grace to be good.

Jesus, so kind and loving, knew we would need many graces to get to Heaven. In His goodness, Jesus gives us graces in the seven sacraments.

For all the important times in our life, there is a sacrament to help us. Baptism makes us children of God. The other sacraments make us grow stronger in the life of grace.

If we commit a mortal sin, the sacraments will restore us to grace. If we hurt our souls with venial sin, the sacraments will make us healthy once more. Whenever we need them, these seven sacraments will fill our souls with grace.

Can we ever begin to know how much love Jesus has for us?

1. _____ grace makes us holy.

2. There are _____ sacraments.

3. Jesus sends us _____ grace to help us stay away from sin.

The Seven Sacraments and Grace: Review Questions

*1. What is a sacrament?
A sacrament is an outward sign instituted by Christ to give grace.

2. How many sacraments did Jesus Christ give us?
Jesus Christ gave us seven sacraments.

3. Where do we find the seven sacraments?
We find the seven sacraments in the Catholic Church.

4. What are the two kinds of grace?
The two kinds of grace are actual grace and sanctifying grace.

5. How do the two kinds of grace help us?
Actual grace helps us be good. Sanctifying grace makes us holy.

6. Who gives us grace through the sacraments?
Our Lord Jesus Christ, the second Person of the Blessed Trinity, gives us grace through the sacraments, through the actions of a priest or bishop.

Baptism

We are all born with original sin on our souls. Original sin is the sin we inherited from our first parents, Adam and Eve. The Sacrament of Baptism removes original sin and makes us adopted children of God.

When you were a baby, you received the sacrament of Baptism. That was a very special day in your life. Baptism took away original sin from your soul.

On the day you were baptized, your parents took you to church, where the priest was waiting for you. The priest asked God to send you His holy grace. Your godmother and godfather made promises for you to God. Because you were too little to speak for yourself, they spoke for you.

Your godparents promised that you would stay away from everything that would keep you away from God. They promised that you would not make anything or anyone more important than God.

As your relatives watched, the priest poured water over your head. While the water was being poured, the priest said a special prayer. "I baptize you in the name of the Father, and of the Son, and of the Holy Spirit."

The water and the words are the signs of the sacrament of Baptism. The water and the words are the signs of what is really happening. Just as water washes away dirt from your body, the water of Baptism cleans your soul. The original sin that you were born with was washed away.

Your Baptism day was a great day in your life! On that day, you became a member of God's family, the Catholic Church. On that day, you became a child of God!

1. When you were a baby, the sacrament of _____ took away original sin from your soul.

2. The _____ and the _____ are the signs of the sacrament of Baptism.

Baptism is the first sacrament that we receive.

We are all children of Adam and Eve. We are all born with Adam's sin.

Before Baptism, you had original sin on your soul. No one with sin on his soul can enter Heaven. Jesus said, "Unless you be born again of water and the Holy Spirit, you cannot enter the kingdom of God."

Baptism made your soul clean. Baptism made you a child of God. Baptism made you a Christian, a follower of Jesus Christ. With Baptism, you became a member of the Catholic Church started by Jesus.

Baptism gave you sanctifying grace. Baptism put God's life into your soul. Baptism made you a temple of the Holy Spirit.

Baptism made my soul holy and pleasing to God! Thank you, Jesus, for the sacrament of Baptism.

1. Baptism made you a _____ of God.

2. Baptism made you a temple of the _____ _____.

Jesus told His apostles to teach all people, "baptizing them in the name of the Father, and of the Son, and of the Holy Spirit."

This was a very important command Jesus gave His apostles. Jesus wants us all to be given every help to get to Heaven.

Original sin had lost for us God's life and love. Baptism gave us a special kind of life. Baptism gives our souls God's life. Baptism opens Heaven for us.

The sacrament of Baptism put a special mark on your soul. This special mark will never go away. This special mark will stay on your soul forever. Baptism allows you to go to Heaven.

After I am baptized, I can receive other sacraments. Soon, I will be receiving two more sacraments. I am preparing to receive the sacraments of Penance and Holy Eucharist. What a wonderful gift I received when I became a member of God's family!

1. Jesus told the apostles to baptize in the name of the _____, and of the _____, and of the _____ _____.

2. Baptism gives our souls God's _____.

3. After I am baptized, I can receive other _____.

Baptism: Review Questions

*1. What does Baptism do for us?
Baptism washes away original sin from our souls and fills us with a special kind of life.

2. What are the signs of the sacrament of Baptism?
The water and the words are the signs of the sacrament of Baptism.

3. How does the priest baptize?
The priest baptizes by pouring ordinary water on the forehead of the person to be baptized, while saying: "I baptize you in the name of the Father, and of the Son, and of the Holy Ghost."

4. Why do we need Baptism?
We need Baptism to wash away original sin from our souls, open Heaven for us, and make us children of God.

5. Do we all need Baptism?
We all need Baptism because we have all inherited original sin from our first parents, Adam and Eve.

6. Can we receive any other sacraments before we have received the sacrament of Baptism?
No, we cannot receive any other sacraments before receiving Baptism.

Penance

We know that Baptism takes away original sin.

Although Baptism takes away original sin, we still have the effects of this sin. This means that we are weak. We may be lazy, or disobedient, or selfish. Because we are weak, we sin. What takes away the sins we commit after Baptism?

Jesus knows that we need more help. Jesus knows that we can be weak and commit sin.

When we are sick or hurt ourselves, our parents take us to a doctor. The doctor will give us the medicine we need to get better.

When we sin, we hurt our souls. Our souls become sick because we lose grace by our sin. Our souls will need a doctor to get better, too.

Kind and loving Jesus is the Doctor of our soul. He gave us a special sacrament to make our soul healthy once more.

The sacrament of Penance is the medicine that will make our souls well.

The sacrament of Penance is the sacrament by which sins we commit after Baptism are forgiven.

1. The effect of original sin is that we are weak, and because we are weak,

   we _____.

2. The sacrament of _____ takes away the sins we have committed after Baptism.

Jesus gave the power to forgive sins to His apostles. Jesus said, "Receive the Holy Spirit. Whose sins you shall forgive, they are forgiven. Whose sins you shall retain, they are retained."

The sufferings and death of Jesus on the Cross have infinite value. That means that the sufferings of Jesus can wipe out all the sins of the world.

By Our Lord's sufferings and death on the Cross, He won this precious gift of forgiveness for us. The apostles handed down the power to forgive sins to the priests. Only God can forgive sins, but He has chosen to do this through His priests.

The priest takes the place of Jesus when he says the words of forgiveness in the sacrament of Penance. Through the priest, our sins are forgiven if we are sorry. Through the priest, it is really and truly Jesus Who is forgiving us.

Jesus will give us every help we need to get to Heaven. Jesus wants us all to enter His heavenly kingdom.

Thank You, Jesus, for giving us the sacrament of Penance.

1. Jesus gave His apostles the power to _____ sins.

2. In the sacrament of Penance, God forgives our sins through the words

   of the _____.

3. Through the priest, our sins are forgiven if we are _____
   for our sins.

4. Thank you, Jesus, for giving us the sacrament of _____.

Jesus once told a story to show how merciful and loving God is.

There was a wealthy man who had two sons. One son left his father's house. He took his share of his father's money and spent it all foolishly.

Soon, the son became hungry and poor. He looked for work but could find only a job taking care of pigs. His food was what the pigs were fed.

The son began to think of his loving father and the beautiful home he left behind. He realized that his father's servants ate much better than he. He realized that his father's servants were treated better than he. He thought, "I have been foolish. I will go back to my father. I will tell him I am not worthy to be called his son, but I will be happy to be his servant."

When the son was walking on the road toward his home, his father saw him from a distance. Quickly he called his servants and said, "Prepare the finest dinner because my son has returned! Bring fine clothes and a gold ring for him and shoes for his feet."

Then the father ran down the road to meet his son.

The young man fell to his knees and told his father, "I have sinned against God and against you. I am not worthy to be called your son."

The father was overjoyed to have his son home. He invited his friends to rejoice with him. "My son was dead and has come back to life. My son was lost, but now he is found!"

When we sin, we are like the foolish son, but when we are sorry, God is a loving Father Who is always ready to forgive us. Through the sacrament of Penance, God will restore to us all that we have lost through our sins. He will always welcome us back with loving and open arms. What a kind and loving Father is God Our Father in Heaven!

1. In the story, we are like the son who was welcomed home by a loving

    _____.

2. God is our loving Father Who is always ready to forgive us when we

    are_____ for our sins.

Penance: Review Questions

1. **What is one of the effects of original sin?**
   One of the effects of original sin is that we are weak. Because we are weak, we sometimes sin.

*2. **What is the sacrament of Penance?**
   Penance is the sacrament by which sins committed after Baptism are forgiven.

3. **Who forgives our sins in the sacrament of Penance?**
   In the sacrament of Penance, God forgives our sins through the words of the priest.

4. **How must we ask for forgiveness, in order to receive it?**
   When we ask for forgiveness, we must be truly sorry for our sins.

5. **What does the story Christ told show us about the love of God the Father?**
   It shows us that God is always ready to forgive us, if we only pray to Him and ask for His forgiveness.

Third Quarter Review

Jesus Is God and Man

Jesus is God. Jesus Christ is God the Son, the second Person of the Blessed Trinity. He came down from Heaven to suffer and die on the Cross to save us from our sins. He became Man to open the gates of Heaven for us.

Jesus chose Mary, pure and sinless, to be His Mother. Jesus chose holy Saint Joseph to be His foster father on earth.

While Jesus lived on earth, He did many wonderful things. Jesus worked many miracles. He cured the sick and raised dead people back to life. He forgave people's sins. Only God can forgive sins.

Jesus worked these miracles to show us that He loves us. Jesus worked these miracles to show us that He is God.

Jesus is fully Man. When Jesus came down from Heaven, He took a body and a soul like ours. He felt everything that you or I could feel, because He had a body and soul like ours. He felt joy and happiness. He felt hunger and thirst, cold and heat. Jesus was like us in everything but sin.

Jesus Christ was not only Man, He was the Perfect Man. He became a man to give us an example of how to act. He taught us how to treat one another. He taught us that we should love one another.

Jesus came to teach us about God, His Father. He taught us how to pray. When we pray, we are talking to God. God wants us to talk to Him often, to be close to Him. This is what the Bible means when we read, "Pray without ceasing."

Jesus Christ is both God and Man. He became a man like us because He wants us to know Him. If we know Jesus, we will love Him and want to serve Him. If we do these things, then one day we will be happy with Him in Heaven!

105

Jesus Suffered and Died, Rose from the Dead, and Founded the Church

Jesus lived with His Holy Family for thirty years. Then, the time came for Jesus to begin His mission to the world.

First, Jesus chose His twelve apostles. He taught them many things about His Heavenly Father's kingdom. Jesus worked many miracles. His most important work was still to come.

Jesus came down from Heaven to suffer and die for our sins. Jesus allowed the soldiers to put a crown of thorns upon His Sacred Head. Jesus allowed the soldiers to cruelly nail Him upon the Cross. Jesus died for our sins on that first Good Friday. He did all this to open the gates of Heaven and win back God's life of grace for us.

After He died, Jesus was buried. The Body of Jesus lay for three days in a tomb. A large stone was placed before the opening, and soldiers were placed outside to guard it. On Easter Sunday morning, Jesus rose glorious and immortal from the dead!

Jesus appeared to His Mother first, then to His friends, and to the apostles. He ate and drank with them. He appeared and disappeared at will. After forty days, Jesus left them to return to His Heavenly Father.

While He was on earth, Jesus started the Catholic Church. Jesus made the apostles the first bishops of the Catholic Church. Jesus made St. Peter the first pope. Our priests and bishops are successors of the apostles. Our Holy Father the Pope is a successor of St. Peter.

Jesus sent the Holy Spirit to guide and protect His Catholic Church. He sent the Holy Spirit on Pentecost Sunday. Today, the Holy Spirit speaks to all of us through the Catholic Church.

The Seven Sacraments and Grace

Jesus gave us a special help called grace to save our souls. There are two kinds of grace. Actual grace is the kind of grace that helps us to be good. We receive actual grace when we pray and do good deeds.

Sanctifying grace gives our souls a new life and makes us holy. The seven sacraments are special and holy gifts from God to help us gain sanctifying grace. Sacraments help us go to Heaven.

A sacrament is an outward sign instituted by Christ to give grace. We cannot see the grace that is given, but we can see the sign of the sacrament. The grace of the seven sacraments brings the life of Christ into our souls.

All sacraments were instituted by Our Lord Jesus Christ. Through the sacraments, Jesus sends the Holy Spirit to pour grace into our souls. He gives us the grace of the sacraments through a priest or a bishop.

The first sacrament we receive is the sacrament of Baptism. The grace of Baptism washes away the stain of original sin on our souls. It makes us a member of God's family, and it makes us a follower of Christ.

Jesus taught His apostles to baptize all people. He taught them to baptize in the name of the Father, and of the Son, and of the Holy Spirit. These are the words the priest said as he poured the water of Baptism over your head. Together, the water and the words are the sign of the sacrament of Baptism.

Baptism takes away original sin. One of the effects of original sin is that we are weak, and can sometimes sin. The sacrament of Penance is the sacrament by which sins we commit after Baptism are forgiven.

When we commit mortal sin, we hurt our soul and lose God's grace. The sacrament of Penance restores the life of grace in our soul. The priest takes the place of Jesus when he says the words of forgiveness in the sacrament. Through the priest, it is really and truly Jesus Who forgives us.

WEEK TWENTY-SEVEN: Day 4

Please review the lessons.

WEEK TWENTY-SEVEN: Day 5

Third Quarter Test.

Fourth Quarter

Confession - Part I

When we break any of God's commandments, we commit sin. Any sin that we commit is called actual sin. There are two kinds of actual sin: mortal sin and venial sin.

Mortal sin is a deadly sin because it takes away God's life of grace from the soul. Deliberately missing Mass on Sunday or stealing a large sum of money, are examples of mortal sin. Adam and Eve's son, Cain, killed his brother Abel. Murder is a mortal sin.

Venial sin is a lesser sin and does not take away God's grace from the soul. Venial sin offends God and weakens our will to obey God. Telling a lie, stealing a quarter, not doing schoolwork or chores, deliberately coming late for Mass are examples of venial sin.

We should try very hard never to commit any sin. All sin greatly offends God. We should hate sin because we do not want to offend our loving God. We should hate sin because no one with sin enters Heaven.

I must do some kind of penance for my sins. If I have committed venial sins and have not made up for them before I die, then I will have to suffer in Purgatory. If I have committed mortal sin and have not asked God's forgiveness before I die, then I will suffer in Hell forever.

Sin is truly a terrible thing and I should do everything I can to avoid any sin, no matter how small I think it may be.

In order to have our sins forgiven through the sacrament of Penance, we confess our sins to a priest. This is called making a Confession.

1. There are two kinds of actual sin, _____ and _____.

2. _____ sin takes away God's life of grace in our soul;

   _____ sin weakens our will to obey God.

109

After His Resurrection, Jesus told His apostles, "Whose sins you shall forgive, they are forgiven them."

Jesus gives Catholic priests the power to forgive sins. Only Catholic priests have that power. In Confession, we tell our sins to a Catholic priest. This is what Jesus wants us to do.

We must remember that Jesus hears what we tell the priest. When we confess our sins to a priest, we are confessing to Jesus. The priest is there to help us. Jesus knows and sees all things. He knows all the sins we have on our souls.

We should tell the priest all the sins we have committed. We cannot keep a secret from Jesus. When we confess our sins with true sorrow, Jesus will forgive them. We must keep away from people who might cause us to sin again.

If we commit mortal sin, a good Confession will bring sanctifying grace back. Jesus gives us grace to keep us from again committing the sins we have confessed. Our soul is pure and beautiful once more.

1. In _____ we tell our sins to a Catholic priest, who has the power to forgive sins.

2. In Confession, Jesus hears our sins, and gives us _____ to keep from again committing the sins we have confessed.

To make a good Confession, we must carefully examine our consciences. That means we try to remember all the times we have broken God's laws.

Before we enter the confessional, we kneel in our pew to prepare. We ask the Holy Spirit to help us. The Holy Spirit will help us remember the sins we have committed.

We ask Jesus to help us remember how many times we offended Him. We tell Him we are truly sorry. We look at the crucifix in church to remember all the sufferings our sins have caused Jesus. We also ask Our Blessed Mother, our guardian angel, and our patron saint to help us make a good confession.

We must have "a firm purpose of amendment." This means we are sorry we have committed these sins and do not want to commit them again.

We tell Jesus we love Him very much. We love Jesus so much, we will try very hard not to sin again.

1. When we prepare for Confession, we try to remember the times we

   have broken God's _____.

2. To have our sins forgiven, we must be truly sorry, and have "a firm

   purpose of _____."

An Examination of Conscience

To prepare for confession I must think about God's Commandments.

I should think of each of the Commandments, see what I am supposed to do, and see if I have done it. If I have broken any of God's laws, then I must tell the priest in Confession.

1) **Adore God.** Did I pray to God each day? Was I reverent in my prayers? Was I good in church? Did I pay attention at Mass?

2) **Treat God's Name with reverence.** Did I always use God's name in the right way? Did I treat the saints and holy things properly?

3) **Keep God's day holy.** Did I go to Mass on Sundays and holy days of obligation? If I came to Mass late, was it my fault?

4) **Obey parents and superiors.** Did I obey my parents? Did I obey right away? Did I treat them respectfully? Did I do my schoolwork and my chores the best way I could? Was I respectful of my elders? the priest? the policeman? Have I been lazy? or careless?

5) **Do not be angry or hurtful.** Have I been good to my brothers and sisters? Did I lose my temper? Did I hurt anyone? Am I kind to everyone I see each day?

6) **Be pure.** Were all my words, looks, and actions good? Was I careful to look only at good movies and shows? Was I careful about what I listened to? Was I careful about what I said? Did I treat my body with respect because it is the temple of the Holy Spirit?

7) **Be honest.** Did I take what did not belong to me? Did I return what I borrowed? Did I return what I found? Did I replace what I broke?

8) **Be truthful.** Did I tell any lies? Did I speak unkindly of anyone?

9) **Be pure in my thoughts and desires.** Did I want to do things I knew were wrong?

10) **Be satisfied with what I have.** Did I want things that I do not have and do not need? Did I pester my parents to buy me things?

If I did not know that something was wrong, then it is not a sin.

Now that I know it is wrong, I must not do it again.

If I remembered or knew it was wrong and still went right on doing it, then it is a sin.

If I committed a serious sin, then I must tell the priest how many times I committed it.

1. To prepare for Confession, I must remember whether I have broken any of God's _____.

2. If I did not know something is wrong, it is not a _____.

113

Confession - Part II

Now that we know how to make an Examination of Conscience, let's learn what else is needed to receive the Sacrament of Penance.

There are five steps to a good confession. Let's go over each step:

1) The first thing we must do before going to confession is to make an examination of conscience. When we prepare to confess our sins, we should go over the questions that we found in the last lesson.

2) After we have remembered our sins, we must be truly sorry for them. If we are truly sorry, God will forgive us. We should be sorry because we have hurt Jesus, Who loves us so much He died on the cross for us.

3) We must try very hard not to commit those sins again. God will give us extra help not to commit sin if we tell Him we love Him, and if we try hard not to commit those sins again.

4) After we have examined our conscience, are truly sorry, and have told God we will try to be good, then we go to the priest and confess our sins to him. We must remember that when we confess our sins to the priest, we are really confessing them to Jesus. When the priest forgives us, it is really Jesus Who is forgiving us.

5) Finally, the priest gives us a penance. Our penance is usually some prayers, like an Our Father and a Hail Mary, that we should say to help make up for our sins. After we leave the confessional, we should go back to our pew and say the penance right away.

1. Before we go to Confession, we must be _____ for our sins,

    and tell God that we will try hard not to _____ them again.

2. After the priest has forgiven our sins in confession, we must say our

    _____ right away.

The confessional is where I tell my sins to the priest. After I have prepared myself and am truly sorry for my sins, I enter the confessional and kneel.

I wait for the priest's blessing, then I make the Sign of the Cross, and I say, "Bless me, Father, for I have sinned. This is my first Confession." (Later, we say, "It has been [one week, one month, or however long] since my last Confession.")

I say, "These are my sins," and I tell Father my sins.

When I am finished, I say, "For these and for all the sins of my past life, I humbly ask pardon, penance, and absolution."

The priest will then talk to me, and I listen carefully to what he says. The priest may ask some questions or he may tell me to do better.

Then, the priest gives me a penance which I say after I leave the confessional. I must remember to listen carefully for my penance.

Next, the priest tells me to say an Act of Contrition. I must say the Act of Contrition loud enough for the priest to hear me. Do I know this important prayer? The Act of Contrition is in the front of this book.

After I say the Act of Contrition, the priest gives me absolution from my sins. My sins are forgiven.

1. In the confessional, I must say the _____ of _____ loud enough for the priest to hear me.

2. After I have said the Act of Contrition, the priest gives me _____ from my sins.

Each night during our bedtime prayers, we should examine our conscience. We pray to Jesus to help us remember our sins. Then we should say an Act of Contrition to tell Jesus we are sorry for our sins. If we do this each day, then it will be easy for us to make a good confession.

While we say the Act of Contrition in Confession, the priest will give us absolution. Absolution means the words of Our Lord's forgiveness: "I absolve you from your sins in the name of the Father, and of the Son, and of the Holy Spirit." This means that God is taking away our sins.

We bless ourselves while the priest says these words. Although we hear the priest, it is really Jesus Who forgives us.

When the priest is finished, he says, "Go in peace." We should remember to say, "Thank you, Father, and God bless you." Then we leave the confessional.

What a great joy! God has forgiven us and He has given us His grace! Our souls are pure and white once again!

Before we begin our penance, we should thank Jesus for His goodness and His great gift to us of the sacrament of Penance.

Then we say our penance as we kneel in the pew. After we have finished our penance, we must try our best not to sin again.

1. When the priest hears our Confession and gives us absolution, it is

   really _____ Who forgives us.

2. In Confession, God _____ our sins and gives us His grace.

116

Confession - Part II: Review Questions

*1. How do you make your confession?
I make my confession in this way:

1. I go into the confessional and kneel.

2. I make the Sign of the Cross and say: "Bless me, Father, for I have sinned."

3. I say: "This is my first confession" (or, "It has been one week, or one month, since my last confession").

4. I confess my sins.

5. I listen to what the priest tells me.

6. I say the Act of Contrition loud enough for the priest to hear me.

2. What does the priest give you after you have confessed your sins and said an Act of Contrition?
After I confess my sins and say an Act of Contrition, the priest gives me absolution, which means God forgives my sins.

3. What must I do to receive absolution?
To receive absolution, I must be truly sorry for my sins, and have a firm purpose not to commit them again.

*4. What do you do after leaving the confessional?
After leaving the confessional, I say the penance the priest has given me and thank God for forgiving my sins.

5. Who forgives sins in Confession?
Jesus forgives our sins in Confession through the words of the priest.

The Mass

Jesus suffered and died on the Cross for us because He loves us. He wished to make up for our sins to God the Father.

His death on the Cross was a gift to God the Father: to adore Him, to thank Him, to make up for our sins, and to obtain graces for us. Our Lord's death on the Cross was a gift to us too: He opened the gates of Heaven to us once more.

The Holy Sacrifice of the Mass and the Sacrifice of Jesus on the Cross are the same. At the Holy Sacrifice of the Mass, Jesus does not suffer and die again. In Holy Mass, Jesus continues to offer Himself to His Father, but in an unbloody way.

When we go to Mass, we are at Our Lord's Last Supper and at His Cross. The Sacrifice of His Body and Blood is repeated for us at each and every Mass. The Mass is the Sacrifice of Jesus on the Cross offered by the priest.

Each day, all over the world, at every hour, Jesus offers Himself in the Mass to God the Father for our sins. When we go to Mass, we should unite ourselves to Jesus in His offering to God the Father. In this way, God will be pleased with us. He will send us sanctifying grace.

What a wonderful gift Holy Mass is! Our Lord Jesus is truly with us at each Mass. We want to be with Him at Mass every day, to tell Him how much we love Him.

1. When we go to _____, we are at Our Lord's Last Supper and at His Cross.

2. The Mass is the _____ of Jesus on the Cross offered by the priest.

At the Last Supper, Jesus changed bread and wine into His Body and Blood. At the Last Supper, Jesus made His apostles the first priests and bishops. He gave them the power to change bread and wine into His Body and Blood.

When the priest begins the Mass, we must remember that he takes the place of Jesus. We must remember that the holiest thing on earth is about to begin. We must be as quiet and respectful as if we were at Our Lord's Last Supper.

At Holy Mass, the priest does what Jesus did at the Last Supper. When the priest says, "This is My Body," at once Jesus is totally present under the appearance of bread.

When the priest says, "This is My Blood," or "This is the chalice of My Blood," Jesus is totally present under the appearance of wine.

This happens at the most important part of the Mass, the Consecration.

We must pay careful attention and be extra good at this very holy part. We kneel quietly and fold our hands in prayer. We look at the priest with reverence.

When the priest raises Our Lord in the Sacred Host, I look at the Host and strike my chest. I say with all my heart, "My Lord and My God!" When the priest raises the chalice, which holds the Precious Blood of Jesus, I bow my head, strike my chest and silently say, "My Lord and My God."

I cannot see Jesus, but He is there, Body and Blood, Soul and Divinity.

1. At Holy Mass, the priest does what Jesus did at the _____

   _____.

2. During the most important part of the Mass, the Consecration, the

   priest changes bread and wine into the _____ and _____
   of Jesus Christ.

We must always be quiet and very respectful in God's house. When we enter, we genuflect on our right knee before we enter the pew. We say a prayer to Jesus Who is in the tabernacle.

At Holy Mass, we say the prayer given to us by Jesus Himself. We say the perfect prayer, the Our Father. We pray, "Give us this day our daily bread." Above all, we ask God to feed our souls with His Heavenly Food.

We thank Jesus for coming to us in Holy Communion. We kneel quietly and pray until the priest has finished giving Holy Communion. We kneel until he places the Blessed Sacrament back in the tabernacle.

At the end of Mass, the priest gives us the Last Blessing. We bow our heads or kneel and carefully make the Sign of the Cross.

When Mass is over, we should not hurry to leave. We should stay and visit with Jesus for a few minutes, since He is still present within us. We should ask Him to bless our family and friends in the coming week. We should tell Him all our cares. This is the best time to pray.

We genuflect when we come out of the pew. We wait until we are out of church before speaking to others. The church is God's holy house and we remember that the angels and saints are there adoring Him.

We must take the graces we have received at Mass and put them to good use in our daily lives. The graces we receive at Mass will help us to be good. The graces we receive at Mass will help us to grow closer to Jesus.

1. In church, we pray to Jesus Who is in the _____.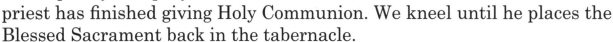

2. The _____ we receive at Mass will help us to be good.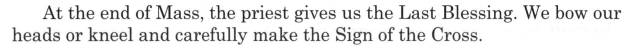

The Mass: Review Questions

1. What is the Mass?
The Mass is the sacrifice in which Jesus Christ, through the priest, offers Himself to God the Father in an unbloody manner under the appearances of bread and wine.

*2. Is the Mass the same sacrifice as the Sacrifice of the cross?
The Mass is the same sacrifice as the Sacrifice of the Cross.

3. Why do we call the Mass an "unbloody sacrifice?"
We call the Mass an "unbloody sacrifice" because Jesus does not suffer and die again, even though the Mass is still the same Sacrifice of Jesus on the Cross.

4. What happens at the Consecration of the Mass?
At the Consecration of the Mass, the words of the priest change bread and wine into the Body and Blood of Jesus.

5. How is Jesus present during the Mass?
Jesus is present during the Mass under the appearance of bread and wine.

6. What does attending the Sacrifice of the Mass give us?
Attending the Sacrifice of the Mass gives us graces for our daily lives.

Holy Eucharist

One day, Jesus told the people, "I am the Living Bread That has come down from Heaven." Another time, Jesus told the crowd that He would give them Food to feed their hungry souls.

Many people did not understand what Jesus meant. The apostles remembered these words at Our Lord's Last Supper, the night before He died.

After they had finished their meal, Jesus took bread and wine and blessed it. Jesus spoke wonderful words. "This is My Body." "This is My Blood." Jesus kept His promise with these holy words. The bread and wine were changed into His Body and Blood!

Jesus became the Living Bread for us all! Only God could do this. Jesus could do this because He is God.

Jesus knew that only with Him could we grow in grace. Jesus became the Food to feed our souls!

Jesus told His apostles, "Do this in commemoration of Me." The Last Supper was the first Mass.

Jesus made His apostles the first bishops and priests. Jesus gave the apostles and all the Catholic priests down to our day this special power. Jesus gave priests the power to work the greatest miracle on earth. Only priests can change bread and wine into Our Lord's Body and Blood.

At each holy Mass, the priest keeps the promise Our Lord made long ago. The priest brings us Heavenly Food for our souls. This Heavenly Food, the Body and Blood of Jesus Christ, we call the Holy Eucharist.

Jesus is the Food for my soul.

The _____ _____ was the first Mass.

The Holy Eucharist is the living Body and Blood of the second Person of the Blessed Trinity, Our Lord Jesus. The Holy Eucharist is His Body and Blood, Soul and Divinity.

The Holy Eucharist is the same living Jesus Who lived on earth about two thousand years ago. The Holy Eucharist is the same living Jesus Who loved the little children. The Holy Eucharist is the same living Jesus Who cured the sick and raised the dead.

The Holy Eucharist is the same living Jesus Christ Who died for our sins on the cross. The Holy Eucharist is Our Lord Jesus Christ.

The Holy Eucharist looks like bread and wine. The Holy Eucharist tastes like bread and wine. But the Holy Eucharist is not bread and wine. The Holy Eucharist is Jesus.

When the priest drinks from the precious cup, he drinks of the Body and Blood of Jesus. What is in the holy chalice looks like wine. What is in the holy chalice tastes like wine. The white Host looks and tastes like bread, but it is not bread. It is the Body and Blood of Jesus Christ.

What is in the holy chalice is not wine. It is the Body and Blood, Soul, and Divinity of Jesus. The Holy Eucharist is God the Son, the second Person of the Blessed Trinity.

The Holy Eucharist is Our Lord, Jesus Christ, God. When I receive the Holy Eucharist, I receive Jesus really and truly and completely.

1. The _____ _____ is the Body and Blood of Jesus Christ.

2. When I receive the Holy Eucharist, I receive _____ really, truly, and completely.

The Holy Eucharist is a sacrament. The Holy Eucharist is a sacrifice.

All of the sacraments were given to us by Jesus Himself while He lived on earth. Jesus gave us the Holy Eucharist at the Last Supper, the night before He died.

Jesus knew He was about to die. Jesus knew He would go back to His Father in Heaven soon. But Jesus wanted to remain with us, too.

Jesus knew we needed His help in a very special way. He knew that without Him, we would find it hard to be good. And so, He gave us the sacrament of His Love, the Holy Eucharist.

We call the holiest part of the Mass the Consecration. That is when the priest says, "This is My Body." "This is My Blood." or "This is the chalice of My Blood."

We know that with those words, Jesus is present on the altar. We know that with those words, the little white Host becomes Jesus. We know that with those words, the wine in the golden chalice becomes Jesus.

We look at Jesus and thank Him for this wonderful miracle. We adore Him. We love Him. We think of Jesus dying for our sins on the cross of Calvary.

1. The Holy Eucharist is a _____ and a _____.

2. All the sacraments were given to us by _____.

3. The holiest part of the Mass is the _____.

4. "This is My _____. This is My _____."

124

Holy Eucharist: Review Questions

*1. What is the sacrament of the Holy Eucharist?
The Holy Eucharist is the sacrament of the Body and Blood of Our Lord Jesus Christ.

*2. When does Jesus Christ become present in the Holy Eucharist?
Jesus Christ becomes present in the Holy Eucharist during the Sacrifice of the Mass.

*3. Do you receive Jesus Christ in the sacrament of the Holy Eucharist?
I do receive Jesus Christ in the sacrament of the Holy Eucharist when I receive Holy Communion.

*4. Do we see Jesus Christ in the Holy Eucharist?
No, we do not see Jesus Christ in the Holy Eucharist because He is hidden under the appearances of bread and wine.

5. What is the Consecration?
The Consecration is the holiest part of the Mass, when the words of the priest change bread and wine into the Body and Blood of Jesus.

6. To whom did Jesus give the power to consecrate the Eucharist?
Jesus gave the power to consecrate the Eucharist to the apostles and to Catholic priests.

Holy Communion

Holy Communion is receiving Jesus in the sacrament of the Holy Eucharist.

Receiving Holy Communion is a very holy thing. When I receive Holy Communion, Jesus comes to me. Jesus, God the Son, makes His home in my soul.

I must clean my soul and make it ready for Jesus. I make my soul ready by going to Confession first. I clean my soul in the holy sacrament of Penance.

I learn my prayers and pray my very best whenever I go to Mass. I am kind to everyone. I am obedient to my mother and father.

When I am good, Jesus sends me graces. Graces make me holy.

I must be very good to receive Jesus in Holy Communion.

It is a very serious sin to receive Jesus if I have a mortal sin on my soul. If I have a mortal sin, I must first go to Confession. There, through the priest, God will make my soul clean once more.

I must learn the rules of receiving Holy Communion properly. If I do not obey these rules, I will displease Jesus. When I have done all these things, then I am ready. Then I can receive Our Lord Jesus in Holy Communion.

1. When I receive Holy Communion, _____ comes to me.

2. It is a very serious _____ to receive Jesus if I have a mortal sin on my soul.

3. If I have a mortal sin, I must first go to _____.

Holy Communion is Jesus in the Sacrament of the Holy Eucharist.

In Holy Communion, we receive the same Jesus Who loved the little children so. We remember how much Jesus wanted the little children by His side. We want to be His children, too.

We will do our very best to prepare for His coming into our souls. That is why we go to Confession at least once a month.

We must not have mortal sin on our souls.

We must not eat or drink anything for one hour before Holy Communion.

We may take water or medicine at any time before receiving Jesus.

It is very important that we obey these rules.

By giving Himself to us in Holy Communion, Our Lord Jesus shows His great love for us. Jesus loves us very much, and wants us to receive Him in Holy Communion during the Holy Sacrifice of the Mass.

THE DISCIPLES OF EMMAUS

1. To prepare ourselves for Communion, we should go to

    _____ at least once a month.

2. We must not eat or drink anything for _____
    _____ before Holy Communion.

3. We must not have any _____ sin on our souls.

On the day I receive Jesus, I prepare my soul with prayer. In church, I am so happy and so good.

When Father raises the Host and chalice of Precious Blood, I pray "My Lord and My God!" I ask Jesus to come to me.

Before Holy Communion, I think of any venial sins I may have committed since my last Confession. I make a good Act of Contrition, and tell Jesus how sorry I am for offending Him.

I walk out of my pew with my hands closed, folded and pointing up to Heaven. I think of Jesus and no one else. I look at the altar and nowhere else. I humbly approach my Lord and my God to receive Him. I open my mouth wide and put out my tongue so the priest can place Jesus on it.

When I have received Holy Communion, I swallow Jesus in the Host right away. I go back quietly to my pew. I am carrying Jesus in my soul and body. I keep my hands folded until I return to my place.

When I am back in my place, I kneel. I close my eyes so that I may better think of Jesus. I might cover my eyes with my hands to help me give all my attention to Jesus.

Now I talk to Jesus. I adore Him. God has come down from Heaven to be with me! I thank Him, for this great Gift of Himself and for all the other gifts He has given me. I ask God's blessing for myself and for others, especially for my family.

I tell Jesus I am sorry for my sins. I tell Him that I love Him with all my heart. Most of all, I tell Jesus that I want to be His child always. I want to be as close to Him each day, as on my First Communion Day. Someday, I want to be with Jesus in Heaven.

1. On the day I receive Jesus, I prepare my soul with _____.

2. When I receive _____ _____, I have Jesus in my soul and body.

Holy Communion: Review Questions

*1. What must you do to receive Holy Communion?
To receive Holy Communion I must:

    1. Have my soul free from mortal sin.

    2. Not eat or drink for one hour before Holy Communion. Water may be taken at any time before Holy Communion.

*2. What should you do to prepare for Holy Communion?
Before Holy Communion I should:

    1. Think of Jesus.

    2. Say the prayers I have learned.

    3. Ask Jesus to come to me.

*3. What should you do after Holy Communion?
After Holy Communion I should:

    1. Thank Jesus for coming to me.

    2. Tell Him how much I love Him.

    3. Ask Him to help me.

    4. Pray for others.

4. Who comes to us when we receive Holy Communion?
Jesus comes to us, Body and Blood, Soul and Divinity, when we receive Holy Communion.

Confirmation

In a few years I will receive another sacrament, Confirmation.

All the sacraments were given to us by Jesus. All the sacraments give grace.

Each time we receive a sacrament, we receive the Holy Spirit. In the Sacrament of Confirmation, the Holy Spirit sends us His special help and strength to fight as soldiers of Christ. We fight as soldiers of Christ to teach about Jesus and His truths.

Confirmation gives us the power to live our faith even better than before. Confirmation helps us to be wise and strong in our faith. Confirmation helps us to understand our Catholic Faith. Confirmation helps us to tell others about Jesus and the Catholic Faith.

Jesus wants everyone in the world to know about Him. The Holy Spirit in Confirmation helps us with this important work. Confirmation gives us the strength to suffer and die for our faith, if we must do so.

One day, I will no longer be a child. Someday, I will be a man or a woman. Then, I will be able to do things that a child cannot do.

ST. TARCISIUS, GUARDIAN OF THE BLESSED SACRAMENT

There are many things I must learn first. It is the same way with my soul. Confirmation helps me to become a grown person in my soul. Confirmation helps me want to know more about God.

1. In the Sacrament of _____, the Holy Spirit sends us His special help.

2. Confirmation helps us to become soldiers of _____.

130

Confirmation is the sacrament through which the Holy Spirit comes to us in a special way. He comes to make us strong soldiers for Christ.

After Jesus returned to Heaven, the apostles were hiding in fear. They were afraid the enemies of Jesus would come after them, too. After the Holy Spirit came, all of that changed.

The apostles were no longer fearful. Instead, they ran into the streets and told everyone they met about Jesus. All of them suffered because of their faith. They were not afraid to suffer or die because they were full of love for Jesus.

That is the power of the Holy Spirit!

Through the Holy Spirit, the apostles became soldiers for Jesus. Through Confirmation, we will be soldiers for Jesus, too.

Through the Holy Spirit, the apostles became strong Christians. The sacrament of Confirmation will make us strong Christians as well.

The Holy Spirit made the apostles wise and full of understanding about Jesus. They were able to explain many things about Jesus Christ and the Catholic Faith that He taught. The Holy Spirit will help us to understand many things about our Catholic Faith that we may not know now.

Soldiers in an army must be brave and strong against the enemy. The Holy Spirit will make me a strong and brave soldier in the army of Jesus Christ.

1. Confirmation is the sacrament in which the _____
   _____ comes to us in a special way.

2. The Holy Spirit will make me a strong and brave _____
   in the army of Jesus Christ.

Confirmation is the sacrament which makes us strong soldiers for Jesus Christ.

We usually receive the sacrament of Confirmation from our bishop. The bishop extends his hands over the head of the person to be confirmed. The bishop prays that the person may receive the Holy Spirit. The bishop then lays his hand on the head. He marks the forehead with the Sign of the Cross.

The sacrament of Confirmation leaves a permanent spiritual mark on our souls. For this reason, we can receive Confirmation only once.

It used to be that when someone was confirmed, the bishop would give him a slight pat on the cheek. This was to show that the person was to be brave and strong.

Sometimes it is not easy to be strong when we must defend our Catholic Faith. Sometimes people are unkind and make fun of others who try to be good. Confirmation gives the grace that will help us in those hard times. Confirmation gives us the strength to obey God.

Confirmation will give us an increase of sanctifying grace. We also receive the seven Gifts of the Holy Spirit. These Gifts are wisdom, understanding, knowledge, counsel, piety, fortitude, and fear of the Lord.

If we work with the graces of this powerful sacrament, then the Holy Spirit will send us His fruits, too. We will learn more about the Gifts and Fruits of the Holy Spirit when we prepare to receive Confirmation.

1. We usually receive the sacrament of Confirmation from our _____.

2. The sacrament of Confirmation gives us the seven _____ of the Holy Spirit.

Confirmation: Review Questions

1. What is confirmation?
Confirmation is the sacrament through which the Holy Spirit comes to us in a special way to help us to be strong Christians and soldiers of Jesus Christ.

2. Who is the usual minister of Confirmation?
The bishop is the usual minister of Confirmation.

3. Why should all Catholics be confirmed?
All Catholics should be confirmed in order to be strengthened to defend our Catholic Faith.

*4. What will Confirmation do for you?
Confirmation, through the coming of the Holy Spirit, will make me a soldier of Jesus Christ.

5. What are the seven gifts of the Holy Spirit?
The seven gifts of the Holy Spirit are wisdom, understanding, knowledge, counsel, piety, fortitude, and fear of the Lord.

Holy Orders and Matrimony

Holy Orders

Up until now, we have learned about the sacraments which are meant for all Catholics to receive: Baptism, Penance, Holy Eucharist, and Confirmation. The next two sacraments are not for everybody.

Holy Orders is the sacrament whereby a man becomes a bishop, priest, or deacon. Only a man can become a bishop, priest, or deacon. Only a man can receive the sacrament of Holy Orders.

To be called by Our Lord to become His priest is a very special honor. There are many reasons why this is so.

The Catholic priest represents Jesus in His Church on earth. Only a Catholic priest has the power to offer the Holy Sacrifice of the Mass. Only a Catholic priest has the power to perform the miracle of changing bread and wine into Our Lord's Body and Blood. Only a Catholic priest has the power to forgive sins in the name of Jesus in Confession.

The Sacrament of Holy Orders gives the man who receives it an increase in sanctifying grace. Holy Orders also gives a special sacramental grace to help the man be a good bishop, priest, or deacon. Holy Orders leaves a permanent spiritual mark on the man's soul. A man who becomes a priest will be a priest forever, because of the permanent mark on his soul.

Boys should pray to see if Our Lord wants them in His priesthood.

In our daily prayers, let us ask Jesus to send us many holy priests.

1. A man who becomes a priest will be a priest _____.

2. Holy Orders is the sacrament by which a man becomes a Catholic

    _____, _____, or _____.

Holy Matrimony

The Sacrament of Holy Matrimony blesses a man and a woman in their life together in marriage.

The husband and wife join themselves together for life. In church, before a priest, they make their marriage promise to God.

Matrimony is a calling from God. Holy Matrimony is the calling that God gave to our own parents.

The sacrament of Holy Matrimony gives the man and the woman the graces they need to make a good and loving home together. This sacrament gives the mother and father the graces they need to raise children according to God's laws.

God wants parents to teach their children to know, love, and serve Him. In this way, they will obtain everlasting happiness in Heaven one day.

Jesus wants everyone in our family to be a saint. The husband should try his best to be like good Saint Joseph. The wife should try her best to be like Our Blessed Mother Mary. The children should obey their parents like the Child Jesus. Together, they should try to live like the Holy Family.

If they do so, then God will bless them with a life of peace and happiness.

1. The sacrament of Holy Matrimony blesses a man and a woman in their

   life together in _____.

2. Matrimony is a _____ from God.

3. God wants everyone in our family to be a _____.

We need Holy Orders to keep the family of Our Lord's Church going. In Holy Orders, God calls men to be bishops and priests. Bishops can ordain, or make more priests through this sacrament. Only a bishop can ordain priests.

We need bishops, priests, and deacons to give us the sacraments. Without them, we would have very little, indeed.

The Sacrament of Matrimony gives Sanctifying Grace to husbands and wives.

The Sacrament of Holy Matrimony keeps our families holy and happy in serving God. God sends the graces to husbands and wives to gain Heaven and to be good examples to their children. God wants parents to help their children to become saints.

Jesus wants us all to know the peace and love He shared in His home. Although the little house in Nazareth was modest, there was no happier place on earth.

We must pray to the Holy Family for our own family. We must pray to St. Joseph for our own father each day. We must pray to Our Blessed Mother Mary for our own mother each day, too. We must ask the Child Jesus to help us be obedient to our parents.

If we follow what Jesus wants, then everyone in our family will be together in Heaven forever.

1. In Holy Orders, God calls men to be _____ and
    _____.

2. In Holy Matrimony, God sends _____ to husbands and wives to gain Heaven.

3. We must pray to the Holy _____ for our own family.

Holy Orders and Matrimony: Review Questions

1. What is the sacrament by which men become priests and bishops?
Holy Orders is the sacrament by which men become priests and bishops.

2. Who can become a priest?
Only a man can become a priest.

3. Does every Catholic man receive the sacrament of Holy Orders?
No, only those men who are called to the sacrament receive Holy Orders.

*4. What is the sacrament of Matrimony?
Matrimony is the sacrament by which a man and a woman bind themselves for life in a lawful marriage and receive the grace to bring up their children to follow the laws of God.

5. Do all Catholics receive the Sacrament of Holy Matrimony?
No, Holy Matrimony is a calling from God, and not all Catholics receive this calling.

Anointing of the Sick

(Extreme Unction)

The last sacrament for us to study is Anointing of the Sick. This sacrament was once called Extreme Unction. Anointing of the Sick, or Extreme Unction, is the sacrament which gives health and strength to the soul, and sometimes to the body, when we are seriously ill or in danger of death. This sacrament is given by a priest to those who are seriously ill or dying.

One day, Our Heavenly Father will call each of us to meet Him. It will be right after we die. We do not know when that day will be, but we must be ready by knowing, loving, and serving God as best as we can.

When we die, our soul will leave our body. Then we will meet Jesus. Jesus will show us all the things we have done, both good and bad.

If we have tried our best to be good, then Jesus will take us to the place He has prepared for us in Heaven.

If we are not ready to go to Heaven, then we will spend some time in Purgatory. People who have not given their love to God and do not have God's life of grace in them cannot go to Heaven and must spend eternity in Hell.

We must pray that we will always love God and stay in His grace while we are living on earth. Only if we die in the state of grace can we go to Heaven.

Jesus gave us the sacrament of Anointing of the Sick to help us at this time. Jesus is so good and loving to give us the sacrament of Anointing of the Sick, or Extreme Unction. Jesus wants to give us every help we need to go to Heaven at the end of our lives.

The sacrament of the _____ of the _____ is given by a priest to those who are seriously ill or dying.

When Jesus lived on earth, He was especially kind to sick people. Jesus gave us a sacrament especially for sick people called Anointing of the Sick.

Anointing of the Sick is also called Extreme Unction. "Extreme" means last. "Unction" means anointing with blessed oil. This sacrament is usually the last blessing with holy oil that is given to a very sick or dying person.

The Sacrament of the Anointing of the Sick prepares us to meet Jesus if we are seriously ill or in danger of death. Jesus sends extra graces in this sacrament to help us at this important time. Anointing of the Sick helps us be ready for Heaven.

When a Catholic is very ill, or hurt in an accident, or very old and ready to die, the priest comes to him. The priest anoints the sick person's forehead and hands with the blessed oil as he prays for the sick person's soul. As he anoints each part, the priest asks God's forgiveness for the sins committed with any of the senses.

The priest then hears the person's confession to forgive any sins he has on his soul. If the sick person is able, then the priest gives him Holy Communion.

If a person is too ill to go to confession or to receive Holy Communion, he may still receive the sacrament of the Anointing of the Sick.

1. The sacrament of the Anointing of the Sick prepares us to meet

   _____.

2. The priest anoints the person with blessed _____.

3. The priest hears the dying person's _____.
   committed.

The sacrament of Anointing of the Sick brings many graces. The graces of this sacrament help a person to be sorry for his sins. It gives him strength to endure the suffering that comes with his illness. If he is dying, the sacrament helps him to prepare for death. It helps him prepare for the meeting with God that comes after death.

This wonderful sacrament takes away venial sins. It takes away mortal sins, too, if the person is too sick to go to Confession.

Anointing of the Sick gives the grace of peace of soul so that a suffering or dying person can worship God with his whole heart. This sacrament strengthens a person against temptations.

Sometimes, this sacrament will make a gravely ill person healthy again. The graces of this wonderful sacrament help the body as well as the soul. If a person receives the sacrament and becomes healthy, he may receive the sacrament again if he becomes seriously ill or when he is dying.

This sacrament prepares our soul to leave this world. It makes us ready to join Jesus, Mary, St. Joseph, and all the angels and saints in Heaven. We will be filled with joy and happiness in Heaven where we will always be happy.

If we have been faithful to Jesus by knowing, loving, and serving Him, then we have His promise of being happy with Him forever in Heaven!

1. The Sacrament of the Anointing of the Sick takes away _____ sin. If the person is too sick to go to Confession, it also takes away

   _____ sin.

2. This sacrament may be received each time a person falls gravely

   _____ or his condition worsens.

Anointing of the Sick: Review Questions

1. Which sacrament prepares us for death?
The sacrament of the Anointing of the Sick prepares the soul for death.

2. What is another name for the sacrament of Anointing of the Sick?
This sacrament is also called Extreme Unction, because it is the last sacrament given to a dying person.

*3. What is Anointing of the Sick?
Anointing of the Sick is the sacrament which gives health and strength to the soul, and sometimes to the body, when we are in serious illness or danger of death.

4. Who may receive the sacrament of the Anointing of the Sick?
The Sacrament of the Anointing of the Sick may be received by those who are seriously ill or dying.

5. May this sacrament be received more than once?
The Anointing of the Sick may be received more than once, whenever a person is seriously ill and in danger of death.

Fourth Quarter Review

Confession

Jesus has given us the sacrament of Penance to forgive the sins we commit after Baptism. Any sin that we commit is called actual sin. There are two kinds of actual sin. Mortal sin is a grievous offense against the law of God, and takes away God's life of grace from the soul. Venial sin is less serious, but offends God and weakens our will to obey God. It is very important to use the sacrament of Penance to free our souls from sin.

To receive the sacrament of Penance, I confess my sins to a priest. I remember that when I confess my sins to the priest, I am really confessing them to Jesus. When the priest forgives me of my sins, it is really Jesus Who is forgiving me.

To receive Our Lord's forgiveness, I must be truly sorry for my sins and I must tell the priest all the sins I remember. To prepare for confession, I must make an examination of conscience.

When I enter the confessional, I tell the priest if this is my first confession, or how long it has been since my last confession. Then I tell him my sins.

To make a good confession, I must make up my mind that I will not commit these sins again. When I have made a good confession, my sins are forgiven me. If I have committed mortal sin, sanctifying grace has been brought back to my soul. I receive graces to help me not to sin again.

Finally, I listen carefully to what the priest tells me. When I leave the confessional, I do the penance the priest gives me.

Mass and the Holy Eucharist

The Holy Sacrifice of the Mass and the Sacrifice of the Cross are the same. Jesus does not suffer and die again, but He offers Himself to God in an unbloody manner. The Sacrifice of Our Lord's suffering and death is renewed at every Mass.

The most important part of the Mass is the Consecration. The priest says the words Jesus spoke at the Last Supper. "This is My Body." "This is My Blood," or "This is the chalice of My Blood." When he says these words, the priest changes bread and wine into the Body and Blood of Jesus.

We must behave our very best at Holy Mass because it is the most important thing that happens in the world each day.

The Holy Eucharist is a sacrifice and a sacrament. At the Last Supper, Jesus gave His apostles very special powers. He made them His priests. He gave them the power to change bread and wine into His Body and Blood. He told them, "Do this in memory of Me."

At each Holy Mass, the priest obeys Our Lord's command. In the name of Jesus, he changes bread and wine into the Body and Blood of Jesus. The Mass is the Sacrifice of Jesus on the Cross offered by the priest.

The Holy Eucharist is the living Body and Blood of Jesus. When we receive the Holy Eucharist, we receive the Body, Blood, Soul, and Divinity of Jesus Christ.

Jesus comes to us in Holy Communion. Jesus, God the Son, comes into our souls. Our souls must be clean and ready for Jesus. We make it clean and ready by receiving the sacrament of Penance frequently.

We must be good to receive Jesus in Holy Communion. We must obey our parents and be kind to everyone in our family. We must learn our prayers and behave our best when we are at holy Mass. We must follow the rules for receiving Holy Communion properly.

Confirmation

In the Sacrament of Confirmation, we receive the Holy Spirit in a special way. Confirmation leaves a lasting spiritual mark on our souls. The Holy Spirit sends us His special help and strength to live our faith better than before. Confirmation makes us strong and perfect Christians and soldiers in the army of Jesus Christ.

Holy Orders

Holy Orders is the sacrament through which a man becomes a bishop, priest, or deacon in the Catholic Church. Like Baptism and Confirmation, Holy Orders leaves a permanent mark on the man's soul. By being ordained a priest, a man receives the power to change bread and wine into the Body and Blood of Jesus in the Holy Sacrifice of the Mass and to forgive sins.

Matrimony

Matrimony is the sacrament that binds a man and woman together in marriage for life. They promise to live together in the love of Jesus and imitate the goodness of the Holy Family. If God sends children, the parents receive graces to teach their children how to know, love, and serve God.

Anointing of the Sick

In the Sacrament of the Anointing of the Sick, the priest anoints a seriously ill or dying person with blessed oil. This brings grace to his soul and prepares him to meet God in the next world. Sometimes, this sacrament will restore health to a dying person.

Fourth Quarter Review Questions

*1. How do you make your confession?

I make my confession in this way:

1. I go into the confessional and kneel.
2. I make the Sign of the Cross and say: "Bless me, Father, for I have sinned."
3. I say, "This is my first Confession." (or, "It has been one week, one month, since my last Confession.")
4. I confess my sins.
5. I listen to what the priest tells me.
6. I say the Act of Contrition loud enough for the priest to hear me.

2. What is the Mass?

The Mass is the unbloody sacrifice of the Cross.

*3. What is the Sacrament of the Holy Eucharist?

The Holy Eucharist is the Sacrament of the Body and Blood of Our Lord Jesus Christ.

*4. What must you do to receive Holy Communion?

To receive Holy Communion I must:

1. Have my soul free from mortal sin.
2. Not eat or drink anything for one hour before Holy Communion, but water may be taken any time before Holy Communion.

*5. What will Confirmation do for you?

Confirmation, through the coming of the Holy Spirit, will make me a soldier of Jesus Christ.

6. What is Holy Orders?

Holy Orders is the sacrament through which men receive the power and grace to perform the sacred duties of bishops, priests, and deacons.

7. What is Matrimony?

Matrimony is the sacrament by which a baptized man and woman bind themselves together in marriage for life and receive the grace to raise their children in the Catholic Faith.

8. What is Anointing of the Sick?

Anointing of the Sick is the sacrament which gives health and strength to the soul and sometimes to the body when we are in danger of death.

Fourth Quarter Test.

Conclusion

We hope you have enjoyed learning about your Catholic Faith. You are in our prayers here at Seton. Please keep all Seton families in your prayers.

May God bless you and your family.

148

Stained Glass Index

Religion 2 for Young Catholics

Answer Key

Week 1: Day 1
1. three
2. Blessed Trinity
3. clover
4. one

Week 1: Day 2
1. Moses
2. miracles
3. Jesus
4. Holy Spirit

Week 1: Day 3
1. Creation
2. created
3. goodness

Week 2: Day 1
1. angels
2. spirits
3. sin

Week 2: Day 2
1. praise
2. messengers
3. guardian angel

Week 2: Day 3
1. good
2. protect

Week 3: Day 1
1. beginning
2. happy, share
3. loving
4. powerful
5. create

Week 3: Day 2
1. goodness
2. Adam
3. soul
4. rib
5. Paradise

Week 3: Day 3
1. parents
2. knowledge
3. grace
4. holy
5. Heaven

Week 4: Day 1
1. fruit
2. Tigris
3. friendly
4. colors
5. perfect

Week 4: Day 2
1. command
2. die
3. disobeying

Week 4: Day 3
1. fruit
2. ashamed

Week 5: Day 1
1. disobeyed
2. grace
3. Paradise
4. health
5. sin

Week 5: Day 2
1. original sin
2. grace

Week 5: Day 3
1. grace
2. original sin
3. Angels

Week 6: Day 1
1. savior
2. Heaven
3. sin
4. suffer

Week 6: Day 2
1. sorry
2. promise
3. Savior
4. sins

Week 6: Day 3
1. man
2. obey
3. original
4. loves

Week 7: Day 1
1. Moses
2. change

Week 7: Day 2
1. happiness
2. Creator
3. Heaven
4. made

Week 7: Day 3
1. sin
2. Heaven
3. Commandments
4. people

Week 8: Day 1
1. worship
2. greatest

Week 8: Day 2
respect

Week 8: Day 3
1. holy
2. Mass
3. rest
4. Lord's

Week 10: Day 1
1. father, mother
2. love, honor, obey
3. love

Week 10: Day 2
1. obedient
2. obeyed

Week 10: Day 3
1. honor, obey
2. obedient
3. obedient

Week 11: Day 1
kill

Week 11: Day 2
1. respect
2. respect

Week 11: Day 3
neighbor

Week 12: Day 1
pure

Week 12: Day 2
belongs

Week 12: Day 3
1. steal
2. honest
3. cheat
4. pay

Week 13: Day 1
lie

Week 13: Day 2
truth

Week 13: Day 3
repair

Week 14: Day 1
married

Week 14: Day 2
1. goods
2. envy

Week 14: Day 3
glad

Week 15: Day 1
1. Incarnation
2. Gabriel

Week 15: Day 2
handmaid

Week 15: Day 3
1. Annunciation
2. Visitation

Week 16: Day 1
1. Man
2. Son
3. stable, inn
4. manger

Week 16: Day 2
1. Savior
2. swaddling
3. adored

Week 16: Day 3
1. Magi
2. star
3. Herod

Week 17: Day 1
Herod

Week 17: Day 2
1. two
2. Holy Innocents

Week 17: Day 3
1. Nazareth
2. priests
3. obeyed

Week 19: Day 1
1. God
2. original sin

Week 19: Day 2
1. second
2. cured
3. God, God
4. miracles, forgiving

Week 19: Day 3
1. see, life
2. loves

Week 20: Day 1
1. body, soul
2. God, Man
3. sin

Week 20: Day 2
1. sin
2. poor, work
3. sufferings
4. Jesus

Week 20: Day 3
1. one another
2. thank
3. love

Week 21: Day 1
1. thirty
2. sins
3. will

Week 21: Day 2
1. Last Supper
2. thorns
3. loves

Week 21: Day 3
1. Good Friday
2. three
3. John
4. Calvary
5. sorry

Week 22: Day 1
1. rise
2. good
3. risen

Week 22: Day 2
1. risen
2. beautiful, glorious

Week 22: Day 3
1. baptize
2. forty

Week 23: Day 1
1. Pentecost Sunday
2. Catholic Church

Week 23: Day 2
1. Pope
2. bishops
3. Pope

Week 23: Day 3
1. Catholic
2. world
3. Grace
4. truth
5. sacraments

Week 24: Day 1
1. Actual
2. Sanctifying

Week 24: Day 2
1. sacrament, grace
2. Jesus

Week 24: Day 3
1. Sanctifying
2. seven
3. actual

Week 25: Day 1
1. Baptism
2. water, words

Week 25: Day 2
1. child
2. Holy Spirit

Week 25: Day 3
1. Father, Son, Holy Spirit
2. life
3. sacraments

Week 26: Day 1
1. sin
2. Penance

Week 26: Day 2
1. forgive
2. priest
3. sorry
4. Penance

Week 26: Day 3
1. Father
2. sorry

Week 28: Day 1
1. mortal, venial
2. Mortal
3. Venial

Week 28: Day 2
1. Confession
2. grace

Week 28: Day 3
1. laws
2. amendment

Week 28: Day 4
1. laws
2. sin

Week 29: Day 1
1. sorry, commit
2. penance

Week 29: Day 2
1. Act, Contrition
2. absolution

Week 29: Day 3
1. Jesus
2. forgives

Week 30: Day 1
1. Mass
2. Sacrifice

Week 30: Day 2
1. Last Supper
2. Body, Blood

Week 30: Day 3
1. tabernacle
2. graces

Week 31: Day 1
Last Supper

Week 31: Day 2
1. Holy Eucharist
2. Jesus

Week 31: Day 3
1. sacrament, sacrifice
2. Jesus
3. Consecration
4. Body, Blood

Week 32: Day 1
1. Jesus
2. sin
3. Confession

Week 32: Day 2
1. Confession
2. one hour
3. mortal

Week 32: Day 3
1. prayer
2. Holy Communion

Week 33: Day 1
1. Confirmation
2. Christ

Week 33: Day 2
1. Holy Spirit
2. soldier

Week 33: Day 3
1. bishop
2. Gifts

Week 34: Day 1
1. forever
2. priest, bishop, or deacon

Week 34: Day 2
1. marriage
2. calling
3. a saint

Week 34: Day 3
1. bishops, priests
2. graces
3. Family

Week 35: Day 1
Anointing, Sick

Week 35: Day 2
1. Jesus
2. oil
3. confession

Week 35: Day 3
1. venial, mortal
2. ill

Like our books?

You might like our program, too. Seton Home Study School offers a full curriculum program for Pre-Kindergarten through Twelfth Grade. We include daily lesson plans, answer keys, quarterly tests, and much more. Our staff of teachers and counselors is available to answer questions and offer help. We keep student records and send out diplomas that are backed by our accreditation with the Southern Association of Colleges and Schools and the Commission on International and Transregional Accreditation.

For more information about Seton Home Study School,
please contact our admissions office.